WELCOMING
AND
AFFIRMING

A Guide to Supporting and
Working with LGBTQ+
Christian Youth

WELCOMING AND AFFIRMING
A Guide to Supporting and Working with LGBTQ+ Christian Youth

Cover and interior design by Emily Harris
Editorial support: Lauren Welch and Erik Ullestad

Print ISBN: 978-1-5064-6498-5
eBook ISBN: 978-1-5064-6653-8

A Companion to **Queerfully and Wonderfully Made**

WELCOMING
AND
AFFIRMING

A Guide to Supporting and
Working with LGBTQ+
Christian Youth

Edited by Leigh Finke

Foreword by Bishop Kevin Strickland

 Broadleaf Books

CONTRIBUTORS

ISAAC ARCHULETA has a master of arts in clinical mental health counseling, and has established a nationally recognized counseling practice devoted to helping the LGBTQ+ community thrive.

CARLA BARNHILL brings more than three decades of working with teenagers to this project. They are among her favorite people. Carla edits and writes and tries to make the world a little better from her home in Minneapolis.

REV. ASHLEY DETAR BIRT is the Pastoral Fellow for Youth and Families at Rutgers Presbyterian Church in New York City. She also serves on the board of More Light Presbyterians, an LGBTQIA+ organization within the PC(USA). Her ministry focuses on children, families, and racial and social justice.

K. AMANDA MEISENHEIMER is a minister and former public-school teacher. She specializes in communication and advocacy for children. She and her two children make their home in Manhattan.

DEACON ROSS MURRAY is the founding director of The Naming Project, a Christian ministry for LGBTQ+ youth, as well as the senior director of the GLAAD Media Institute. He is a deacon in the Evangelical Lutheran Church in America, with a calling to LGBTQ+ advocacy and ministry between the LGBTQ+ and faith communities.

GERMONO TOUSSAINT is a multi–award-winning playwright, composer, and producer, and an African American, same-gender-loving, ordained minister. He is the founding artistic director of A Mile In My Shoes Inc., and one of the founding playwrights of the Obie Award–winning The Fire This Time Festival. Due to his upbringing in the often-contradictory world of basement parties and the black church, his work focuses on how people navigate the sacred and the profane, the flesh and the spirit, or the natural and the supernatural.

CONTENTS

FOREWORD

Bishop Kevin L. Strickland,
Bishop of the Southeastern Synod—ELCA

The book of Esther has one of my favorite lines of Scripture: "for just such a time as this" (Esther 4:14). As I read *Welcoming and Affirming*, these words rang loudly for me. For such a time as this, we in the church can be benefactors of this book. In many ways, I wish my pastors when I was a youth would have had such a resource, and even I, when serving as a parish pastor, would have benefited from such a treasure of riches.

One might ask, Why the need for such a book? Even more so, why, when so many churches have signs reading "All are welcome"? It is one thing to say all are welcome and a completely different thing to do the work of making a safe and affirming faith community for people who identify as LGBTQ+.

Welcoming and Affirming is a book for such a time as this. It will educate congregations as they support and work with LGBTQ+ youth. It is a necessary and life-saving book. A 2017 GLAAD/Harris poll found that as many as 20 percent of eighteen- to thirty-four-year-old persons identify as LGBTQ+, compared to 12 percent of thirty-five to fifty-one-year-olds. Today's teens are expected to continue that trend.

That means one in five kids (if not more) in America's churches identifies as LGBTQ+.[1]

Research also shows that LGBTQ+ youth who say religion is "very important" to them are 38 percent more likely to attempt suicide than those who say religion is "less important."[2]

What these numbers tell me is that we—all of us in America's churches—have an opportunity to save lives. This book can show us how to do that. We have an opportunity to learn how to ask questions. To learn what questions to ask. To learn how to listen to the stories of our LGBTQ+ siblings in Christ. To learn how better to welcome them fully into a safe place. To tear down stereotypes around sexual orientation and gender identity that so often get in the way of us seeing each person as a beloved child of God.

One of the greatest lessons I ever learned is that you will never look into the face of someone God does not love. That extravagant, expansive, and nonbinary love of God, who created each of us in God's own image. That image which doesn't fit into any box of human construction or binary limitations.

As a Lutheran, I believe in justification. If that is the case, I believe that we are justified by God's grace and not by our own doing. We live daily in that grace.

This expansive grace can be made ever more visible, but not with a church sign reading "All are welcome." Rather, it is by the intentional work we do as the church to truly show all people what inclusive grace looks and feels like. This book does just that. It will support LGBTQ+ teenagers in their journey to know who and whose they are, while congregations learn more about this beloved part of the body of Christ.

John Bell, in his hymn text "Will You Come and Follow Me," gives us these words:

> Will you love the you you hide if I but call your name?
>
> Will you quell the fear inside and never be the same?
>
> Will you use the faith you've found to reshape the world around, through my sight and touch and sound in and you and you in me?

As a married, gay man who is currently serving as a bishop in the ELCA church (Wow! I never thought I would be able to say any of those three things!), I was haunted for years by Bell's words before I was able to come out. I grew up in this church and never questioned God's love for me. But I did question God's people's love, acceptance, and welcome for me. I wasn't ready for my own questions, much less questions from others.

For such a time as this, I give thanks to God that a book like *Welcoming and Affirming* now exists. I pray that it provides the knowledge that we have all been created, called, and welcomed by God's abundant grace. That it quells the fear we have within and guides us to further use our faith to reshape the world. I pray that those who use this resource as pastors, teachers, church professionals, youth leaders, and more will see what a tool for ministry this can be. This book asks us to learn, listen, and walk together. It's exactly what we need in this church and our world. It literally can save lives and nurture souls.

For such a time as this, God has called each of us, in our fullness, to be our full selves and to live abundantly in life-changing grace. May it be so for all!

A QUICK NOTE ON LANGUAGE

QUEER

We're using the term *queer* as shorthand for the entire LGBTQ+ community. This includes all sexual orientations outside of heterosexuality: gay, lesbian, bisexual, pansexual, asexual, and more. Queer also includes gender identities beyond the binary gender structure of male and female: transgender, nonbinary, genderqueer, agender, and more.

Of course, that's a lot of unique people being covered in a single word. Not everything in this book applies to every queer person. But there are many experiences that are common for all queer people of faith, and those are the experiences this book will address when using this word.

CHRISTIAN

When we use the word *Christian* we're talking about the whole culture of Christianity. All of it.

There's so much diversity represented in that word that we'd need twenty volumes to get into the details of the various expressions of the Christian faith and how they approach LGBTQ+ inclusion in the church. So assume that if you and your church call yourselves Christians, then we're talking about you.

All right then, let's get to it.

A BRIEF INTRODUCTION

It's no secret that the church hasn't always been a loving environment for queer people. Or that queer teens have felt isolated from their Christian communities and families. In fact, for most of history, the church hasn't treated LGBTQ+ people with basic human kindness. This is a problem, and it needs fixing.

Maybe that's why you picked up this book. To help you fix this problem.

Because maybe you've heard negative comments from your church community about LGBTQ+ people. Or noticed that your church is unclear about how it welcomes and accommodates queer people of faith. Maybe you're a part of an affirming congregation but you're just not sure if you're doing the right things to truly support your queer youth.

Whatever need you're trying to meet, we know you want real, helpful, honest information and guidance on how to affirm, support, and engage with the queer teens in your youth group, neighborhood, school, or community.

Before we dive in, we need to make a few things clear about what you won't find in this book:

1) If you're looking for discussion, debate, or answers to theological questions about LGBTQ+ identity and Christianity, you won't find it here. We are starting from the belief that LGBTQ+ people are beloved children of God, full stop. So we're not going to do a point/counterpoint with all the clobber verses or mount a series of arguments about why you *should* welcome and affirm queer teens. There are lots of books out there engaging in the theological side of this conversation. We've listed several in the back of this book.

2) If you're in the process of sorting out your own ideas about sexuality and gender and faith, that's wonderful, and we encourage you to do the necessary hard work and self-examination on that front. But that's also not what this book is for. This book is meant to help your church become a place

where queer kids know they are loved, accepted, and included. That's it. That's the goal. Like everything else in youth ministry and education, it's not about you. It's about them.

3) While we have gathered the data and paired it with advice and wisdom from experienced youth workers, LGBTQ+ advocates, and queer young adults, you won't find quick and easy answers here on working with queer teens. That's because these questions aren't hypothetical. They are real questions based in the experiences of actual people. The answers affect real teenagers, some of whom are desperate for help. Not to put too fine a point on it, but these questions are literally life-and-death for some young Christians.

Every student you work with will have their own story to tell, and it probably won't line up neatly with a one-size-fits-all response. People—and faith—don't work that way. You know your students and your context best, so consider this a solid starting point from which to learn how you can approach each person with love, care, and compassion.

Here's what you will find:
An honest discussion about some of the biggest issues facing LGBTQ+ youth today. You'll find practical recommendations for building an affirming faith community. You'll hear stories and advice from real queer people of faith. You'll find hope and inspiration and even some fun. At the same time, you'll wrestle with disturbing data on suicide, homelessness, and risky behavior among queer youth. You'll be shown the dangers of conversion therapy in all its forms. You'll be asked to have some uncomfortable conversations. That's the work ahead.

As you go through this book, we invite you to hold a posture of open heart and hands. Read to deepen your understanding and challenge your perspective. Read to learn, and then act on what you learn. Read to make changes in your faith community. Read to bring healing and grace and hope to the kids in your care.

WHAT IS LGBTQ+, AND WHAT DOES IT LOOK LIKE?

CHILD FUNNY **ASEXUAL** NONBINARY
BIRD-WATCHER GAMER **BISEXUAL** ARTIST
ATHLETIC LOUD
GAY **QUEER** DOG RESCUER
ACTOR SON SCIENTIST
BANJO PLAYER
PARENT COUCH SURFER
ACCOUNTANT **LESBIAN TRANS** CEO
BAKER **MOTHER SHORT**
CAT LOVER **BARISTA**

Yes, there are a lot of initials in the acronym, and yes, the list seems to get longer all the time. But behind each of those letters is a real, live person hoping to be seen and understood. In a 2018 study, LGBTQ+ youth identified themselves with more than one hundred gender identities and sexual orientations.[3] The list is constantly evolving to fit new expressions of queerness, including terms you have probably never encountered.

If you're unfamiliar with basic language of queer identities, it might be beneficial to read through our short glossary at the back of this book. Knowing these terms and definitions will greatly help your interactions with the LGBTQ+ teens in your group. (It's also going to help this book make a lot more sense.)

YOU CAN'T DEFINE LGBTQ+.

Every queer identity is different, and each is expressed differently by individual persons. Just as we don't expect every straight woman or man to wear the same clothes, speak the same way, or have the same hobbies, we need to recognize that queer people don't fall into equally restrictive categories. An LGBTQ+ person is just that—a person—unique, wonderfully complex, and worthy of love.

There's no shame in not understanding what every initial in our queer acronym means. Given that LGBTQ+ identities receive very little representation in popular culture and Christianity, why would you? Still, there is a growing community of real-life LGBTQ+ teens and adults expressing their identities and orientations in an ever-expanding queer language across multiple media platforms. That means teenagers are seeing a broader range of options for how they want to express themselves and the adjectives that best describe them. When you're a kid who knows there's something unique about you, there's a lot of comfort in finding a name for it.

WHAT DOES LGBTQ+ LOOK LIKE?

The first step in answering this question is to be aware of your own biases. What do you *expect* a queer teenager to look like? What stereotypes have you bought into, and why do you have that perception? Where does it come from?

There are some common stereotypes:
* a certain style of dress
* involvement in the arts or drama
* interest in queer TV shows and movies
* rainbow apparel or tattoos or hair or just rainbow everything

Of course, these *are* sometimes indicative of a young person's emerging queer identity, and it's certainly not wrong for anyone to express themselves in any of these ways. But each person will express their queerness differently, sometimes subtlety, sometimes boldly. Some will move through queer clichés searching for their space (just like all teens), and some will have no outward expression at all. A young person's external characteristics should never be the ground for an assumption of queerness, nor should they be a disqualifier ("Well, you don't *dress* like a lesbian").

When you're working with queer kids, it's crucial to do self-reflection. How much do you know—actually know—about queer culture? (There's no right or wrong answer here. Just be real with yourself.) How often do you engage with a queer young person? Do you feel comfortable having conversations about LGBTQ+ topics, or do you feel anxious just thinking about it? Wherever you're at, remember that grace abounds!

Don't make assumptions about your preparedness or about the young people you work with. Getting to know a culture or group different than your own takes time and effort. It means learning a new language, media, symbols, icons, and behaviors. The more familiar you are with these aspects of queer culture, the better you can engage with your LGBTQ+ youth.

So how do you do that? Here are a few ideas:

★ Familiarize yourself with LGBTQ+-affirming Christian communities and organizations (there are many and we have listed some in the back of this book to get you started). Notice the issues they discuss, the challenges they face, the places they find support.

★ Learn LGBTQ+ terms and definitions.

★ If you already have LGBTQ+ youth in your group, pay attention and ask thoughtful questions. What are they watching? Who are they listening to? What language do they use for themselves? Remember that each teenager will have their own answers to these questions.

★ If you don't have many in-person LGBTQ+ interactions, ask other adults you trust about their experiences, or look online. Which social networks, forums, and online groups are LGBTQ+ teens a part of? Who are their icons and influencers?

Queer culture is rapidly changing and growing. Learning about the LGBTQ+ people in your community will be a lifelong journey. But building a bridge toward queer youth in your work communicates volumes to them. It tells them you see them, you value them, and you care about their lives. That's a big deal.

DON'T OVERLOOK INTERSECTIONALITY.

One other thing to keep in mind when discussing LGBTQ+ topics is intersectionality.

The word *intersectionality* was coined in 1989 by lawyer, activist, and professor Kimberlé Crenshaw to describe the multiplying effects of racism and sexism faced by women of color.[4]

Today, the term is used more broadly to identify the overlapping, compounding effects of multiple types of discrimination facing a particular person. For example, a queer person of color with learning disabilities may encounter a combination of racism, ableism, and anti-queer discrimination. That experience will look very different from that of an urban cisgender gay male. As Audre Lorde said, "There is no hierarchy of oppression," but it is crucial to understand that the lived experiences of individual queer people are not the same.[5]

When engaging with a teenager in your congregation, be aware of the intersections they live in, and ask yourself:

★ What other obstacles might this teenager face in combination with their gender identity or sexual orientation?

★ How is their life affected by these factors, and is that experience something I can relate to?

★ How can (or can't) I help them address these factors?

You will not be able to solve every issue in the lives of queer youth (and no one is asking you to). But recognizing the intersectional realities of oppression will help you better understand a teen's unique experience.

A FEW RECOMMENDATIONS

If you want to understand the breadth of LGBTQ+ identity and experience:

* Remember that queer kids are whole people and not defined by just one aspect of their identity. Some people incorporate queerness into all aspects of their lives. Others don't.

* Ask what media, online communities, and technology platforms queer kids are using.

* Maintain a nonjudgmental mindset as you listen and learn.

* Language: know it, use it, value it. Ask for and accept definitions, pronouns, and names.

* Ask: What makes you feel seen? How can I support you better?

* Don't learn alone! Build your own support cohort or education network. The more people with you in this, the better.

* Listen, learn, and believe what your queer youth tell you. Be a champion, not a questioner, of their voice.

A FINAL THOUGHT

Having diverse expressions of gender and sexuality within your faith community is an unqualified good. When an LGBTQ+ young person joins your group, look for how they make your whole group better. How do they challenge stereotypes and assumptions? How do they reveal another side of God's creation? How do they embody a unique expression of love? The more familiar you are with LGBTQ+ culture, the better you will be able to recognize and honor these qualities.

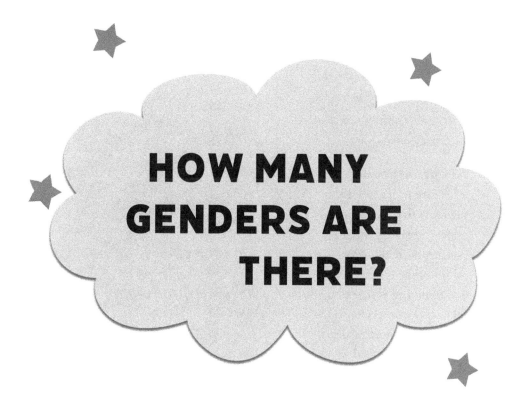

HOW MANY GENDERS ARE THERE?

If you grew up in any era prior to, you know, right now, you were probably taught that there is a simple answer to this question. And that answer is two.

But science has helped us discover that there is so much more to gender than we previously thought. Now we recognize that there is a difference between biological sex and the culturally created and highly variable concept of gender. We know that both sex and gender are more expansive than simply "male" and "female." And far more complicated.

The World Health Organization defines gender as:

> The socially constructed characteristics of women and men—such as norms, roles and relationships of and between groups of women and men. It varies from society to society and can be changed.

Let's point out a few key phrases here. Gender . . .

Is socially constructed
Varies from society to society
Can be changed

Gender is not an "either/ or" situation. It's not a rule book that everyone follows. Rather, gender is a spectrum of behaviors, attitudes, appearances, and more, and is expressed differently in every individual regardless of biological sex. Gender is influenced by when someone is born, where someone is born, family values, social environments, sexual orientation, and countless other factors.

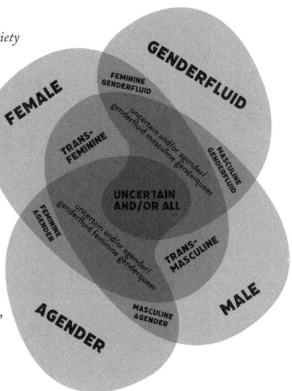

THE SOCIAL NATURE OF GENDER

For many people, the idea that gender is a changing social construct goes against what they believe about how men and women should look and act. But if we consider the idea of static genders critically, it's not hard to see the gender binary start to unravel.

It helps to look at the ways many of our modern understandings of gender have been shaped over the last couple centuries.

★ High-heeled shoes were created for aristocratic men in France to show off their legs.

★ Women were considered to have higher libido than men until the nineteenth-century Protestant church changed the script.

- Babies and toddlers wore dresses and skirts until the 1930s, regardless of birth sex.
- In the 1940s, computer programming was considered a woman's job.

Take a look at this quote from a magazine article printed in 1918:

> The generally accepted rule is pink for boys, and blue for girls. The reason is that pink, being a more decided and stronger color, is more suitable for the boy, while blue, which is more delicate and dainty, is prettier for the girl.

> —*Earnshaw's Infants' Development*

That's right, pink used to be the Man Color. Who knew? The color switch aside, this quote is a good reminder that our ideas about gender shift over time and across cultures. The idea that there has always been one way to be female or male is just a myth. Today's "universal gender characteristics" were almost all created in the past one hundred years.

A RECOMMENDATION

There are reasons many people hold to a binary understanding of gender, including how they understand the biblical account of creation (more on this later). But it's important, at the very least, to listen to the stories of people who exist outside of that binary.

- There are millions of genderqueer, transgender, and nonbinary people, many of them Christian and looking for affirming faith communities. If your views on gender are limited to man and woman, challenge yourself about why you hold this view, and what it means for the queer youth in your church (they *are there!*).

A FINAL THOUGHT

You don't have to understand queer identities in order to affirm and accept queer youth. Genderqueer, transgender, and nonbinary are authentic human experiences, and have been so for as long as humanity has been on this planet.

One of the most damaging things you can do is invalidate another person's experience of gender, regardless of what you believe. Listen to and believe your youth, even if you can't imagine feeling the way they do. We are called to love all, regardless of our experience.

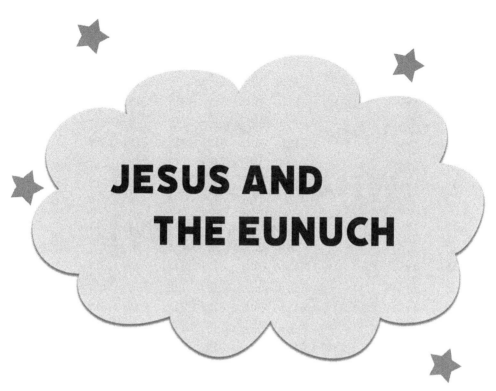

JESUS AND THE EUNUCH

Eunuchs, as theologian Austen Hartke describes, were "the gender-diverse people of the ancient world" who "lived outside the boundaries of sex and gender." Basically, queer people. Many people today don't realize that there are queer people in the Bible.

But Jesus knew this, and to him, the presence of queer people was extremely no big deal. In Matthew, Jesus tells his disciples, "For there are eunuchs who have been so from birth, and there are eunuchs who have been made eunuchs by others, and there are eunuchs who have made themselves eunuchs for the sake of the kingdom of heaven. Let anyone accept this who can" (Matthew 19:12). It really doesn't get clearer than that.

Later, in Acts, an angel instructs Philip to join the chariot of the Ethiopian eunuch. Philip does, and after the two read Scripture on their journey, the eunuch asks Philip to baptize him into Christ. Philip does not say, "Sorry, I cannot bring into Christ a person who doesn't fit contemporary gender structures." Rather, Philip baptizes the eunuch immediately, making them one of the very first Christians (Acts 8:26–40).

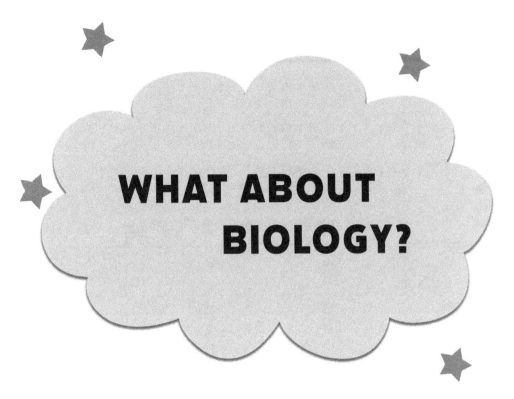

WHAT ABOUT BIOLOGY?

You've probably heard all of the arguments: There are two biological genders, two sexes for the purpose of reproduction. You're either XX or XY—there aren't any other options. So how can someone be anything other than male or female? How could they be born one sex but claim another one later?

To answer these questions, we first have to define some terms, using the *Our Whole Lives* sexuality education curriculum:

- ✦ **BIOLOGICAL SEX:** The physical sex characteristics— genitals, reproductive organs, hormones, and chromosomes—a person is born with. Roughly 98 percent of people are born male (XY) or female (XX), but around 1.7 percent of people are born intersex (for example, XXY), meaning they have a combination of male and female sex characteristics. That's about the same number of people who are born with red hair.

- ✦ **GENDER IDENTITY:** A person's internal sense of their gender. The majority of people have a gender identity that matches their biological sex, but for some people, these two things are very different. Think of gender identity as who your brain tells you you are. Cisgender people are those for whom biological sex and gender are the same. Transgender people are those for whom they are different.

✦ GENDER EXPRESSION: The way a person reveals or expresses their gender identity through clothing, voice, behaviors, hobbies, mannerisms, etc. Ironically, many of the ways we express gender have nothing at all to do with gender. Clothes, colors, hairstyles—they are all neutral until a culture decides to assign them a gender. Still, these external expressions of gender are one of the primary ways our brains put people into gender categories.

✦ SEXUAL ORIENTATION: A person's romantic, emotional, and sexual attractions to others. This is unrelated to biological sex and gender. Anyone can be heterosexual, homosexual, bisexual, pansexual, asexual, etc.

A WORD ABOUT INTERSEX

While we're not going to spend a lot of time on intersex people in this book, it's important to take a second to note what intersex biology means. Intersex includes a host of variations in which a person is born with or develops sex characteristics that blur the binary lines of biology, including the following:[6]

✦ Klinefelter Syndrome, in which a person is born with an extra X chromosome, making them XXY. Though most people with Klinefelter Syndrome grow up as cis-men, some develop atypical or female gender identities.

✦ Ovotestes, in which a person's gonads contain both ovarian and testicular tissue.

✦ Androgen Insensitivity Syndrome (AIS), in which a person is born with ambiguous genitals that are neither fully male nor female. In patients with AIS, surgery is often done to make the genitals functional or to delineate the person's gender.

Being biologically intersex is neither a guarantor nor a prerequisite for a queer identity. Just because someone is born intersex doesn't mean they will develop a queer sexual orientation or gender identity.

Intersex is also not related to transgender identity. A large majority of transgender people are born with a clear biological sex. Intersex, like all biological sex, doesn't define someone's gender identity or sexual orientation. But it does help us understand that all individuals are unique, and that genetics does not obey, and never has obeyed, our rules.

AND YET . . .

Even with all of that laid out, some people remain convinced that being queer is a choice, an anomaly, a problem to be solved. But nothing could be further from the truth.

Some people argue that queerness is wrong because it is unnatural and not observable in any other species on earth. This is false. Homosexual behavior has been documented in more than 450 species.[7] Anthropologists have been studying the issue since 1952 and have found homosexual behaviors in all primates and in every human society they have studied.[8] There are intersex animals, animals with more than two sexes, even animals that change their sex depending on the circumstances. In many ways, human beings are far less queer than other members of the animal kingdom.

The argument that someone is always, from birth, one of two genders simply doesn't hold up in history, culture, or science. Gender and sex in humans and across the animal kingdom are much more complicated than "male" and "female." Biology is an essential part of our identities, but it certainly isn't the only part of our being.

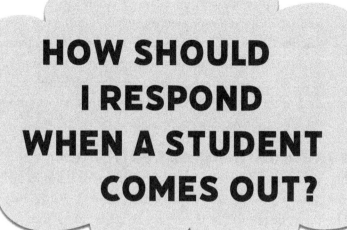

HOW SHOULD I RESPOND WHEN A STUDENT COMES OUT?

One of the great privileges of youth ministry is when a young person invites you to be part of a major life experience. Whether they're sharing the excitement of a first kiss, getting into their first-choice college, choosing their first tattoo, or sharing the heartache of their parents' divorce, it's a big deal when they seek you out for these conversations. That's when you know you've done the hard work of establishing a healthy, trusting relationship with them.

Having a queer student come out to you demonstrates that same level of trust. Still, it might not be a conversation you've had before or one you feel entirely comfortable with. There's a lot to unpack when a student comes out, so it's understandable that there will be all kinds of questions and emotions swirling around in your brain—and in theirs too. Your job isn't to get all of those questions answered right away. It's to be a safe, caring person.

Here's what that looks like:

RECOGNIZE THE COURAGE IT TAKES TO COME OUT.

When a student comes out, they are claiming a new identity for themselves and inviting you into their process of figuring out what that will look like. It's possible their announcement is coming after a long time of questioning, but maybe not. Regardless, make sure your words, your facial expressions, and your energy communicate your understanding of the strength it takes to share something so important, and that you're here for whatever comes next.

CELEBRATE THIS MOMENT WITH THEM.

It's a big deal to come out—a milestone and a turning point in the lives of many queer people. If it seems appropriate, tell them you're excited and happy for them. Be proud that they took this step, and tell them so. Even if *you're* not ready to celebrate this news, recognize the step *they* are taking. And don't ever treat coming out as a crisis or a problem to be solved.

DON'T EDITORIALIZE.

Avoid adding your own commentary about your own assumptions. Never say you suspected, or "I always wondered." Don't say "I'm completely stunned." Your previous assumptions aren't helpful in this circumstance. And frankly, they didn't matter before, and they're irrelevant now.

Similarly, never say "still" or "anyway" when expressing affirmation. Saying "God still loves you" or "I/Your family will love you anyway" conveys the message that being queer is something that rightfully should cause a diminishment of love.

REALIZE THAT THIS IS JUST A STEP.

Coming out may be this young person's first step in exploring their queer identity and orientation. While it's very likely they have thought about this decision for a while, they might not have any additional information to share. They might not be ready to tell anyone else, or you might be the tenth person they've told. Be ready to let your student lead the conversation and give space for whatever emotions they express.

ESTABLISH EXPECTATIONS ABOUT CONFIDENTIALITY.

Someone's sexual orientation or gender identity is not your information to share, and there are very, *very* few circumstances in which it is okay to out a queer person to *anyone*.

As such, it's critical for you to be aware of your church's protocol, practices, and safe-sanctuary policies when it comes to confidential conversations and to not make any promises about privacy that you can't keep. And be sure to ask your student who they have shared with and what information they want to keep private.

Always keep in mind that depending on the student's family situation, telling their parents could create a host of problems. Don't let your assumptions about their family sway your decision. If a student tells you they aren't ready to tell their parents, they have their reasons. This isn't a conversation you should force (see: "What Can I Tell the Parents?" on page 171). You can talk with your queer student about how *they* want to tell others, but unless they specifically tell you otherwise, this is *not* your information to share.

It's important to prepare for a conversation like this, even if you don't think you currently have any LGBTQ+ students in your group (and you probably do). Whenever your group gathers, be intentional about creating a safe space for teenagers to be who they are. Establishing this secure foundation will make it easier for all of your students to be the people God made them to be.

RECOMMENDATIONS

If you're not ready to have this conversation:

* Get ready. You're gonna have it.

* Push yourself into uncomfortable territory.

* Remember that this is not about you. It's about a young person reaching out for acceptance and belonging.

If you're confident about having this conversation:

★ Respond with immediate affirmation, acceptance, and an expression of God's love.

Addy, 28:

Have I come out at church? No, and there are two reasons for that: 1. I've seen what the church does with people that do come out (it's not pretty) and 2. I haven't personally come out to my own family, and they are actively involved in my church. Growing up, I didn't stick to just one church, I went to a few different denominations and areas just to see what the difference was. Unfortunately, every single one had the same views of LGBTQ+ people. It was strange, because they would all have lenient views on drinking, light drug use (as in marijuana), and even premarital sex, but God forbid Jake having a crush on Stephen. It was a bit frustrating, so I never wished to be "out" in the church.

Mary, 26:

Honestly, my church leaders were so loving toward me. I came out as bisexual to my head pastor and his wife and it never once affected how they treated me or my involvement in that community. No one tried to "convert" me, no one shamed me, no one made me feel I wasn't good enough. I was able to hold a position of influence in the youth group as a worship leader/mentor and was able to teach the youth. I still held my position as a corporate worship leader as well. Not once did they out me to anyone without my consent. I know that I could have had it a lot worse and I am so thankful for their love and support.

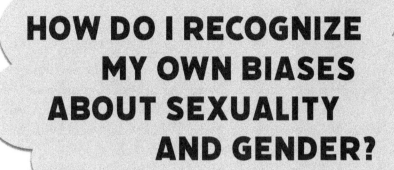

HOW DO I RECOGNIZE MY OWN BIASES ABOUT SEXUALITY AND GENDER?

Let's start with the facts: You have biases. We *all* have biases. We're born and raised in specific environments, families, and cultures that affect our viewpoints and shape our brains. There's nothing wrong with having biases, and no shame in acknowledging our biases. They are just there. But acknowledging they exist is the only way to work toward overcoming them.

In order to see your biases, start by simply identifying who you are. For example, you might be a white, middle-class, able-bodied, cisgender, suburban, married man. If so, you have a set of experiences that are different from an African American lesbian, a Latinx nonbinary immigrant, or a disabled white man experiencing homelessness. That you view the world differently makes sense and is not surprising or a failure.

Acknowledging our biases is only the first step in being faith leaders who are inclusive and affirming. We must also consider how our individual life experiences have affected our thinking and assumptions.

Ask yourself:

★ What advantages have I had because of my identity? What disadvantages?

★ What obstacles have I faced and/or avoided simply because I was born into a certain family, neighborhood, or body?

★ What might someone of a different race, gender, or orientation experience that I haven't?

Obviously, none of us has control over the identities and culture we were born into. But we absolutely do have control over how we leverage those identities and cultures and how we engage with people who are different from us. This is especially true for people of faith. We are called to consider others as valuable as ourselves. We are followers of Jesus, who preached about welcoming strangers and caring for those who suffer. As a youth leader, you have the great privilege of creating spaces of welcome and care for the LGBTQ+ kids in your community who are too often treated as outsiders.

As you consider your personal biases, think too about the biases your church might have. What assumptions are made about queer kids that might be keeping them from being fully welcome? How can you break through some of those and build bridges between your church and your LGBTQ+ students?

RECOMMENDATIONS

If you want to recognize and work through your personal biases, then:

★ Participate in a bias training program through your denomination or a community organization.

★ Undergo a self-assessment to discover your blind spots and implicit biases (for example, the Harvard Implicit Association Test, or the Implicit Bias Test by the American Bar Association).

★ Learn about the harm of your biases through LGBTQ+ people in your denomination.

★ Do your own work: Seek educational resources to learn about a contrasting perspective, especially those related to your implicit biases. Read testimonies, stories, and biographies of those from completely different backgrounds than yours.

★ Don't look to your youth for answers. It's not their responsibility to educate their elders.

If you want to challenge biases among your staff/group, then:

★ Create a learning campaign. Encourage your pastoral team, youth volunteers, and staff to take an implicit bias test.

★ Host Q&As, read books as a group, watch TED Talks, etc.

★ Take your small group through a season on learning about different perspectives on sexuality and gender.

A FINAL THOUGHT

Recognizing and working through your biases can be hard, lonely work. You will likely feel vulnerable, unnerved, or totally out of your comfort zone as you do so. You might upset friends, family, or colleagues by sharing what you learn. You might be shocked by the changes you see in your heart and viewpoints. Nevertheless, exploring and overcoming your biases is a beautiful journey toward growth and maturity as a leader. And this work is a gift to your vulnerable queer kids.

A *FINAL* FINAL THOUGHT: WHEN YOU MESS UP

Even with all the research and learning, you're still going to have unconscious biases. You're going to make mistakes, whether saying the wrong thing, making the incorrect assumption, or simply forgetting what you've learned. This is just part of being human. In fact, we have a whole chapter about just that (see "What If I Get It Wrong?" on page 94).

Eli, 28:

Negative thoughts toward the LGBTQ+ community are so common that it's almost impossible to get to adulthood and not have any bias against queer people. So, don't feel bad or defensive if you find yourself making assumptions about how queer people look, act, or live. Just recognize that you have those pre-existing biases and then work to eliminate them. Honestly, most LGBTQ+ people I know, including myself, have dealt with internalized homophobia/transphobia. I spent years occasionally thinking, "I can't possibly be a lesbian, I like my long hair" or "I don't want to be a lesbian, lesbians are so mean and scary." That's what society, church, and my family taught me. They probably learned it from someone before them.

The LGBTQ+ community is as varied as any other community—some people are kind, others not so kind, some people are vocal and proud of who they are, some are more reserved, some are even ashamed. Some are drag queens and activists, some are accountants and airline pilots, some are teachers, some are outlandish, some are as regular as anyone else you meet. Some "don't look gay." We come from every type of background, family, and circumstance. So, if you think about the LGBTQ+ community as one big unit, you probably just need to meet more LGBTQ+ people. I think seeking out queer people and getting to know about their lives is the best way to break any biases you have.

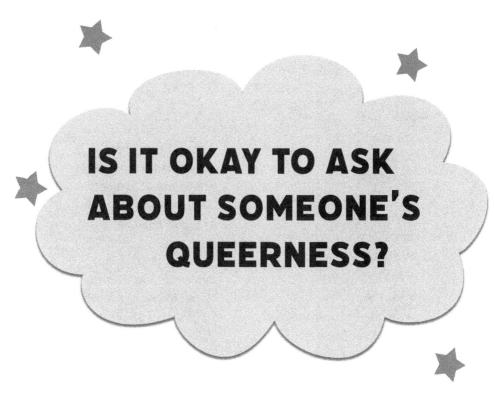

IS IT OKAY TO ASK ABOUT SOMEONE'S QUEERNESS?

Questions about a person's identity can be tricky to navigate, especially with young people who might not be ready to—or even know how to—answer these questions. Leading, assumptive, or inappropriate questions can quickly break a teenager's trust. However, avoiding questions altogether can come across as disinterest in learning about and from the young people in your care.

So yes, ask questions, but recognize that some questions build trust and others erode it.

CONVERSATION DOS

* ✦ Aim for open-ended questions. Questions with no "right" answer give teenagers the space to process and share where they're at. Avoid asking questions that can only be answered with a yes/no or questions you think you know the answer to. Avoid: "Are you trying to tell me something with that outfit?" Try: "Tell me about those cool earrings I've seen you wearing." Frame your questions in a way that allows a teenager to share authentically. Use your

questions as tools to better understand your student, not a way of getting your opinion across.

★ Ask about your students' pronouns and names, as well as the identity markers they want you to use (for example, gay, bisexual, queer). This is a tangible way of showing you value and respect what they're sharing with you. Doing this with all of your students normalizes conversations about identity and gives queer kids a gentle on-ramp for coming out when they're ready.

> **People do not have "preferred" names and pronouns. They might be different from their given or legal name and assumed pronouns, but changing names and pronouns is not a "preference"; it's an affirmation of one's true self.**

★ When a student comes out to you, focus your questions on their experience, not yours. For example, ask how you can help them feel supported and encouraged in your youth group. What concerns do they have that you can address?

★ Clarify the boundaries of your communication. This is good standard practice with all of your students. Ask what they're comfortable with you sharing—and with whom—and what they'd like you to keep private. Ask them who else they've talked to. Make sure you know and communicate your sharing obligations before making promises (more on this on page 166).

CONVERSATION DON'TS

★ Never (*ever*) ask someone directly if they are LGBTQ+, even if you "suspect" or have "heard from others." When, how, and to whom a person discloses their identity/ orientation is solely and always their decision. Forcing a teenager to talk about their identity in ways they aren't ready for robs them of the opportunity to figure out how they want to do this. That step is essential for their own growth and sense of themselves.

★ Do not ask about sex or make assumptions about a student's sexual orientation or experiences. You wouldn't do this with any other teenager in your youth group, so don't do it with the queer kids either.

★ Avoid commenting on changes you've noticed in the way a student dresses or what their body looks like—and don't let your other students do it either. Many teenagers choose to change their look—some do so frequently— and you don't want to make erroneous assumptions at a delicate point in a young person's queer self-realizaiton.

★ Don't ask questions out of curiosity. If you have generic questions regarding LGBTQ+ identities and issues, a teenager should not be your primary source of information. Never make your students feel responsible for educating you or answering your "I've always wondered . . ." questions.

★ Don't assume everything is terrible. Discovering and exploring one's queerness can be a truly joyful experience for a teenager, so be careful not to automatically treat a student's sexuality or gender diversity as a problem or a crisis. Queerness should never be portrayed as a sacrifice or as a life with less potential than any other. Queer people live wonderfully complete lives with diverse and meaningful stories, relationships, and experiences.

Once a student comes out to you (we'll talk in depth about this conversation starting on page 27), you can ask more precise questions. Some starting points:

★ Determine their physical, emotional, and mental safety. Find out who else they are processing this with, and offer resources for finding other trusted adults who can provide guidance, if necessary.

★ Find out how they're feeling about their faith and their church. Be ready to offer support here as well. Refrain from making unhelpful judgments or assumptions about their feelings toward religion or faithfulness.

★ Offer to pray with them. Don't be offended if they say no. Ask simply and honestly about how you and the church can be praying for them.

Be mindful of a young person's comfort level when discussing certain topics. Don't take it personally if they prefer not to answer certain questions. Make sure they know they always have the right to *not* answer any question or discuss any topic. LGBTQ+ kids don't owe you—or anyone else—anything they're not ready to share. Practice active listening skills by verbally acknowledging what they share, repeating their answers back to them, and asking clarifying questions.

A FEW NOTES FOR ANY CONVERSATION WITH A QUEER PERSON

★ Avoid the use of the word *preferred* when discussing names and pronouns. It implies that queerness is an optional and chosen identity, and not a revealed identity.

★ Don't second-guess anyone: "Are you sure?" "How do you know?" *Never, ever* frame questions like this. We're not sure we can say this strongly enough. Most likely, a teen has thought long and hard before coming out. And even if they have, it's possible that they're still not 100 percent sure. And that is 100 percent okay. Uncertainty-provoking questions invalidate a teen's experience and can generate anxiety, shame, or doubt. Instead, frame your questions in a way that supports a teen in being exactly where they are in their journey.

Never put conditions on your (or God's) approval with words like "anyway" or "still" or "regardless." Phrases like "God still loves you," "You're welcome here, regardless," or "I think you're great anyway" will be felt for what they are: indications that there is something wrong. A teen's identity or orientation should never be presented as a disqualifier for love and acceptance. God's inclusive love is unconditional. Yours should be too.

Aliya, 19:

> Even when I started to frequent more progressive and affirming places of faith, the language was often, "I still love you, it doesn't make any difference, it doesn't matter to me," which was good, but still framed it as I was lucky to be tolerated. What I wish church leaders had understood was that it was something I needed to have celebrated. I needed an adult to look me in the eyes and tell me they were proud of me, that they loved me (without the pesky "still"), and that they were there for me in whatever I needed going forward. I needed someone to acknowledge that this was part of God's design for me, and it was beautiful. Neutral language is good, positive language is better. Instead of striving for tolerance, strive for celebration.

WHY DOES LANGUAGE MATTER SO MUCH?

Within the LGBTQ+ community, words matter. Profoundly so. And supportive leaders and allies need to understand this and speak accordingly. Thoughtful language shows respect, acknowledgment, and acceptance. This means using a person's authentic name over their birth name. It might mean using different pronouns for a young person than the ones they were given as a child.

These changes are not mere technicalities. And no one chooses to change their name or pronouns to be a burden on others. Instead, this is about a queer person striving for an authentic life. Hearing these words from someone they trust is incredibly powerful. Conversely, using incorrect language will feel insensitive and hurtful, whether it's done on purpose or not. Making passing remarks or jokes about queer people, repeatedly forgetting to use a person's pronouns, using someone's previous name instead of their real name—these things aren't harmless mistakes. They speak volumes about the value you place (or don't place) on a queer person's identity.

We get that this is new territory for many people and that even the most well-meaning among us will use the wrong words now and then.

But even when people don't intend to be cruel, making excuses for being less than intentional with words can add to the pain it causes. Those excuses tend to fall into three categories:

1) Avoidance ("I'm never going to say anything because I'll get it wrong.")

2) Defensiveness ("This is hard to remember; they should be more understanding!")

3) Defiance ("I'll say what I want; it's just words.")

What do these excuses have in common? They are all about *you*, the adult in power, and not the vulnerable kid seeking affirmation. When you get the language wrong (and you will—that's okay), just say you're sorry and acknowledge your desire to get this right.

THIS IS NEW TO YOU, NOT TO YOUR TRADITION.

The use of proper, and changing, language is actually a deeply Christian concept. Throughout Scripture, God uses names and labels to reflect a person's identity, mark a change in their life story, or call them into something new. Here are just a few examples:

✦ ABRAM/ABRAHAM AND SARAI/SARAH: When God spoke the promise of new life and blessings over this couple, God marked this event not with a ceremony or celebration, but with something much more enduring: a name change. Abraham and Sarah's new identities and futures were embodied through language.

✦ JACOB/ISRAEL: God honored Jacob's literal fight with God with a name change. Israel means "he struggles with God." This identity has marked an entire nation for literally thousands of years.

✦ SIMON/PETER: Peter was the first disciple to boldly acknowledge Jesus as God in flesh. Jesus recognized this step of faith by declaring Simon (meaning "God has heard") to be called Peter (meaning "rock").

LANGUAGE TELLS OUR STORY.

The words we use for ourselves honor the unique people God created us to be. We want the names we use outwardly to reflect who we know we are inwardly. Our words and names point not just to who we have been, but to who we are becoming.

For many LGBTQ+ people, finding their words, names, and definitions is a tough process. Especially during adolescence. Teenagers (queer or not) spend this age exploring and discovering who they are. Being queer adds another step, often fraught with guilt and shame, to this journey. When everything else feels confusing and uncertain, hearing others adopt affirming language like names and pronouns can create a sense of stability. Using and repeating this language back to a young person shows them that

1) you're listening to them,

2) you care about them, and

3) you value their experience (just as you would with any student in your group).

HOW DO I LEARN THE LANGUAGE?

Non-LGBTQ+ people may get anxious hearing—let alone being expected to use—language they don't understand or simply aren't used to. At this point, you might be flipping back to the LGBTQ+ glossary or additional recommended resources. And while that wouldn't be the worst thing to do (definitely learn your terms), there are many other steps you can take right now to grow in your understanding and use of language:

★ Listen to the words a young person uses to describe themselves. Ask what pronouns they use. Then use them (this will take practice).

★ Remember that avoiding harmful and inappropriate language is not the same thing as using affirming language. While you should certainly be doing the former, don't stop there with a half-hearted "That's good enough, right?"

* Don't roll your eyes at the growing LGBTQ+ list. Each letter stands for an adjective that defines actual people. And while these words can't fully encapsulate a human being, they are important markers for many queer youth.

* Acknowledge that an individual's language—identifying markers, names, and pronouns—might change. Someone might come out bi, then later identify as gay. Someone might adopt they/them pronouns, before moving to she/her or he/him. Queerness is a process, and nothing is static.

* This is true for every teenager. But the risks for LGBTQ+ teens are higher than for their straight/cisgender counterparts. Patience and love throughout the process are crucial for avoiding negative outcomes.

* Avoid binaries about gender (boy/girl) and sexuality (straight/gay) whenever possible, and not just with queer youth. Even if you don't have LGBTQ+ students in your group at the moment (that you know of), practicing nonbinary language now gets everyone used to it and makes the group far more welcoming for all teenagers.

* Start to take note of how often you use binary gendered language, and make an effort to reduce or eliminate it from your work with youth. Phrases like, "All right, guys, listen up!" or "Ladies and gentlemen . . ." can feel unwelcoming to gender nonconforming youth, and frankly, it's usually unnecessary. It encourages the idea that a young person *must* fit perfectly into one or the other category to participate in your group and can create shame for those who don't, or who think they might not, fit into the neat categories. Try "Hey, folks, time to settle down!" or "Friends, it's time to welcome our guest speaker."

Whew! That was quite a list. Fear not. Take a breath. You don't have to be perfect by next Wednesday night. What you *do* have to know is that definitions, pronouns, names, and other identity-related words matter deeply to the person experiencing them. Don't underestimate the power of a pronoun to let a teenager know they are seen, heard, and welcome in your group.

A FINAL THOUGHT

If you want queer kids to feel accepted and cared for, using queer-affirming language is one of the simplest places to start. Whether you're in an LGBTQ+-affirming church or not, you'll need to be intentional about creating a group that's welcoming to LGBTQ+ youth. Unfortunately, you can't really ride the fence on this. You can either use affirming language and be an ally to LGTBQ+ youth, or not. Without that language, it's unlikely LGBTQ+ teenagers will feel welcome and safe.

That means you might need to lead the way on helping students, volunteers, and other adults in your church become more tuned in to language. You can get them on board by communicating that you aren't doing this to be trendy or because someone is forcing you. Instead, show them that language is one of the ways we acknowledge, honor, and love people. It's a missional approach to understanding one another.

> *Sal, 19:*
>
> What a lot of straight/cis people don't understand is that LGBTQ+ (especially youth who have experienced homophobia) are constantly on guard, both for homophobia and affirmation. What comes across as a minor detail to you is a tip-off for us. For a lot of members of the trans community, something as simple as the phrase "he or she" instead of the singular "they" is a red flag that you don't recognize nonbinary genders, and they can't be honest with you. Things as simple as using the full acronym instead of "gays," offhandedly condemning homophobia, or use of that singular "they" pronoun can give us hints that we can trust you. Even if we never come out to you, they mean a lot to us.

WHAT DOES IT MEAN TO BE TRANSGENDER?

Transgender is (like all letters in the LGBTQ+ acronym) an adjective, not a noun. The word describes a person who has the sustained experience of gender dysphoria.

> **gender dysphoria:** *noun*
> A condition in which somebody feels that they were
> born with the wrong sex *(Oxford)*

Gender dysphoria can be experienced in a number of ways, and the word *transgender* is often used as an umbrella term for all gender nonconforming queer identities. Which means that transgender men and women, as well as nonbinary, agender, or genderfluid individuals may all identify as trans. This distinction is important when looking at data about trans youth.

Only about 0.6 percent of the total population identifies as transgender (this number is self-reported, however, and demographers think the actual number is likely up to two times higher).[9] Among youth ages thirteen to eighteen, the number who self-identify as gender nonconforming or trans is 10 percent.[10]

TRANS IS NOT A FAD

Transgender people, like same-sex attracted people, have always existed. There's never been a society or culture at any point in history that has not had trans and gender nonconforming members. While we are not going to spend time here arguing for the existence of trans people or their right to self-actualization and expression (see: Trans/GNC Resources under Additional Resources), here are three quick facts to reinforce the point:

* The Roman emperor Elagabuls ruled from 218 to 222 CE. From childhood, Elagabuls was known to live beyond the boundaries of male gender norms. As emperor, Elagabuls offered huge sums of money to any doctor who could "equip him with female genitalia."[11]

* Many Native American cultures considered gender nonconformity a spiritually significant trait.[12]

* Evidence of genderqueer people can be found in the Bible. In the Old Testament book of Deuteronomy, right after laws about returning your neighbor's sheep and ox when they escape, are prohibitions on gender nonconformity. "A woman shall not wear a man's apparel, nor shall a man put on a woman's garment" (Deut 22:5). The full purpose of this prohibition is debated, but enforcing gender binaries in society has forever been part of the response to queer and trans people.

WHY ARE PEOPLE TRANSGENDER?

The source of gender dysphoria—the feeling that one's gender does not match one's birth sex—has been studied for decades. Its cause is . . . chromosomal? Or maybe related to the development of the brain in early childhood? Or environmental factors? Yeah. There are lots of theories. But as of now, the precise cause of gender dysphoria remains unknown.

And that's okay. The *why* is not actually a significant question when it comes to how one interacts with queer youth. The answer is: We don't know why some people are cisgender and others are transgender, nonbinary, or agender, *and it doesn't matter*. Just like we don't know precisely why some people are gay, lesbian, or bisexual. What matters is that God's creation is beloved, and your job is to reflect that love to all.

THE DATA ON TRANS YOUTH

Trans youth often face particular difficulties that their heterosexual and cisgender peers do not:

1/2 of trans youth are prevented from using a restroom or locker room at school that matches their gender identity.

2/3 of trans youth are not addressed by their name.

4/5 of trans youth are not addressed by their pronouns.

2/3 of trans youth cannot express their gender identity in school.

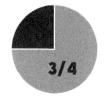

3/4 of trans students feel unsafe at school.

Human Rights Campaign

The data on trans and gender nonconforming youth goes on like this. In almost every area of life, genderqueer youth find barrier after barrier that keeps them from being themselves and being seen as themselves. And the results are clear—mentally, socially, and physically. Queer young people who do not get support from family, faith groups, and social networks are more depressed; more anxious; more likely to smoke, drink, and use drugs; and more likely to commit suicide than their straight or cisgender peers.[13]

VIOLENCE AGAINST TRANSGENDER PEOPLE

Rates of physical and sexual violence against transgender people are alarming.

 31% of trans youth experienced violence in the past 12 months, compared to 10% of cis youth

 24% of trans youth were threatened or injured with a weapon at school in the past 12 months, compared to 5% cis youth

The Trevor Project

That doesn't mean every transgender teenager is at risk of physical or sexual violence. But it does mean that transgender teenagers can carry a deeply rooted fear with them every day.

RECOMMENDATIONS

Many trans teenagers face specific discriminations and difficulties in their daily lives, and no matter what you do, you can't promise a safe, risk-free life for your trans youth. But you can make *your church* a place where they can let down their guard and feel safe. For a queer young person to know there is at least one safe, affirming, loving place to go where they will be seen and addressed and allowed the freedom to live is invaluable. Truly.

SOME WAYS YOUR CHURCH CAN BE SENSITIVE TO TRANSGENDER YOUTH

★ Always, always, always use the authentic name and pronouns of your trans youth.

★ And don't say: "It's hard, it'll take time, it's weird . . ." Just do it.

- Make bathrooms gender neutral all the time, for everyone. If that's not possible, figure out how you could create at least one gender-neutral bathroom in the building during youth gatherings.

- Group students for activities by anything other than gender. Make groups based on grades or birthdays or the alphabet or any number of other categories.

- Run through your tried-and-true stories and anecdotes to weed out any that play into gender stereotypes or identities.

- Instead of single-sex small groups or activities (like "Guys Movie Night" or "Girls Bible Study"), offer topical small groups or interest-based activities that can include all gender expressions.

A FINAL THOUGHT

It's crucial to be aware of the risks faced by trans and gender nonconforming youth. But it's just as important not to reduce youth to these risks. Many queer youth live full and happy lives. And studies show that with support and love from parents and supportive adults, transgender youth have outcomes essentially the same as cisgender youth regarding health, safety, and happiness.

WHAT DOES IT MEAN TO TRANSITION?

The experience of gender dysphoria leads some transgender and nonconforming people to make changes that allow them to live a more authentic life. Making these changes is part of a process called *transitioning*.

There are lots of ways—some very big; some very, very small—in which an individual can undertake gender transition. These actions are grouped into three categories:

1) Social transition: changing one's appearance, behavior, name, and language

2) Legal transition: using courts, etc. to recognize one's gender in legal documents such as driver's license, Social Security card, and birth certificate

3) Medical transition: using hormones, surgery, and other interventions to alter physical body and appearance

All forms of transition are complex and can take a year or a lifetime. Transition is a highly individual process, and not every trans or nonconforming person goes through all of the processes. Some people may not transition at all (this does not mean their trans identity is not real).

Transitioning is not a decision taken lightly, and the process is often lengthy, with each step requiring lots of discernment, work, and support from others.

For queer youth, most of the opportunities to transition are social and not permanent. Social transition can begin at any point in life, starting from one's earliest years. Youth who have affirming family, however, may begin the use of puberty-blocking hormones, allowing a young person to delay the permanent physical effects of puberty (delaying puberty is done for many reasons, and does not normally cause any negative health outcomes).

> Gender-confirming surgery is almost never performed on individuals under age eighteen. In almost all cases, the only medical transition that is allowed for youth is puberty-blocking hormones, a life-saving option for many people struggling with gender dysphoria.

Common social transition steps:

- ★ Coming out as trans or nonconforming (this is sometimes referred to as disclosing)
- ★ Using a different name
- ★ Using new personal pronouns
- ★ Wearing different clothing
- ★ Changing hairstyles
- ★ Wearing makeup, or no longer wearing makeup

A young person's decision to transition can seem sudden or rash to other people. When a child expresses a desire to transition, parents and church leaders might have concerns about their motives or decision-making process, or wonder if this is just a phase the child will grow out of. For some teenagers, experimenting with gender expression might just be part of trying on some new identities. This doesn't make every kid who explores gender trans.

But trans identity is real, and gender dysphoria is not a phase.

When a teenager says they want to transition, it's a huge deal. Perhaps a *humongous* one, for that child.

It's likely they've been thinking about it for a long time. They know the risks involved and are showing tremendous courage in making the changes they need to feel at home in their body. If a teenager tells you they want to transition, know that they are trusting you with one of the biggest decisions they'll ever make.

Don't tell them they'll grow out of it. Celebrate their courage, and help them!

TALKING WITH PARENTS

Many parents, even supportive ones, will have questions and concerns about their child transitioning. They might worry about their child experiencing regret or taking irreversible action before they are ready. They might worry—rightfully so—about their child's safety in school, at church, and in the community. Parents might wonder if they have failed somehow or be embarrassed about how their family and their child will be perceived by others.

Before talking with the parents, do your research on the realities of transitioning. Know the stages and steps, and be ready to share them. Gather a list of helpful resources, including websites, parent support and advocacy groups, and therapists and counselors to give parents a place to start. (See "Additional Resources" on page 190.)

When talking with parents, be sure to listen to their concerns while reminding them that the priority is their child's well-being. Remind them that the best way to love and ensure a safe and productive future for their child is to affirm and support them, not to seek to change them or deny who they are. We'll talk more about conversion therapy on page 66, but for now, please know that it does not work, and it leads to tragic outcomes.

RECOMMENDATIONS

If the family is questioning or rejecting transition:

* ✦ Help them understand the many steps in the process, and communicate your support for their teenager and their family.

- Encourage holistic discernment. Transition rarely jumps straight to medical intervention. Families have time to move through this process at a pace that works for their teenager.

- Explain how decisions made out of fear can cause a breakdown of the parent-child relationship. When a teenager feels unsupported by their parents, they may seek out harmful ways of coping. Lack of support can also increase feelings of anxiety, depression, thoughts of suicide, and drug use. If parents are struggling with their teenager's gender identity, encourage them to seek counseling and support for themselves.

- Give space for and mediate healthy conversations between parents and teenagers.

If transition is underway:

- Advocate for smart, safe, thoughtful decision-making.

- Provide a safe space for parents to grieve. Yep, this can be rough for parents. It's okay for them to feel sadness and a sense of loss even as they love and support their child.

- Be ready to talk with your student about their fears and worries about their own safety and changes in their relationships with family or friends.

- Know your limits. Trans teenagers will benefit from a professional, trained counselor or therapist. Have some names ready to recommend (outside of the church).

- Be willing to talk to your other students, your volunteers, and other church leaders about your student's pronouns, name change, and any other issues the student wants you to cover. It's tremendously helpful to take on some of this work for your trans student.

- Advocate in your church community on behalf of the family. They have plenty to think about without having to walk other people through this process too. Provide listening posts or forums on LGBTQ+ issues where church members can learn and ask questions.

★ Protect your student's emotional and physical safety. Keep information confidential unless you have explicit permission to share it. Pay attention to how your trans student is treated by the rest of the group, and intervene when necessary.

★ As counterintuitive as it sounds, don't make a bunch of sudden and drastic changes to your program that draw attention to your trans student. Trans and nonconforming youth don't want to be the center of attention or the cause of a whole bunch of new policies and practices. This is all the more reason to make changes to bathrooms, language, and gender expectations well before you ever have a student come out.

A FINAL THOUGHT

The decision of when and how a teenager should transition is not yours to make—or even weigh in on. Your role is to care for the student and help them and their family go through this process in a healthy, positive way. Be an advocate and a mediator, not a barrier. Foster honest communication that builds up families and individuals.

Marc, 20:

> To be transgender is to feel, at some level, fundamentally disconnected from the gender your parents told everyone you were, whether that is how you look, or how the people around you see you, or how you act. It means that, if you are told you are a girl, you would rather be counted among the boys, or vice versa. For me personally, this also means I would like to wear suits to church, and participate as a deacon, which is a men-only role in my church. This is not because I can't do this as a woman, because there are many unofficial and church-affiliated groups that do the same things as deacons and are run by women, but because I feel like it is right for me, and I'm supposed to do this. It's difficult to explain, but it is like a divine calling sometimes.

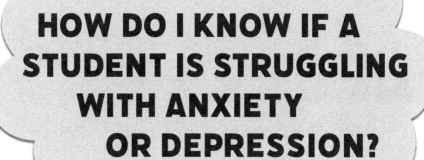

HOW DO I KNOW IF A STUDENT IS STRUGGLING WITH ANXIETY OR DEPRESSION?

Mental health is one of the most pressing issues facing teenagers today. Diagnoses of anxiety and depression are occurring more frequently and at increasingly younger ages. And while mental health disorders are increasing for teenagers in general, LGBTQ₁ teenagers arc at an even higher risk than their straight ir cisgender peers of experiencing anxiety and depression at some point in their lives. Consider the data related to mental health among LGBTQ+ teenagers and adults:

LGBTQ+ adults are more than twice as likely as heterosexual adults to experience a mental health condition.

National Alliance on Mental Health

77% of LGBTQ+ teenagers surveyed reported feeling depressed or down during a given week. More than 70% report feelings of worthlessness and hopelessness.

Human Rights Campaign

95% of LGBTQ+ teenagers surveyed had trouble sleeping in the course of a week. Sleep deprivation is a well-documented cause and symptom of several mental health conditions.

Human Rights Campaign

 The prevalence of feeling sad or hopeless was nearly three times higher among gay, lesbian, and bisexual youth than their heterosexual peers.

Human Rights Campaign

The numbers are even worse among LGBTQ+ teens who are also part of other minority groups. Compared to their nonminority LGBTQ+ peers, minority LGBTQ+ teenagers have higher rates of depression, yet are less likely to pursue therapy and counseling.[14]

Faith also does not offer protection for LGBTQ+ young people. A 2019 study found that gay and lesbian college students who said religion was "very important" to them were 38 percent more likely to have considered suicide than those who said religion was "somewhat" or "not very important."[15]

"WHY CAN'T YOU JUST FEEL BETTER?"

Historically, the church and society in general haven't done a great job addressing mental health concerns. When young people do reach out for help, the response from adults can often be less than helpful.

"They're just doing it for attention."

"Everybody thinks they have anxiety these days."

"All teens are moody. It doesn't mean they're depressed."

"Just pray about it!"

"If you had enough faith, you wouldn't have [insert mental health condition]."

Even if these awful comments are well-intended, it's not uncommon for people to put the blame for anxiety or depression on the person suffering.

The idea that people can just power through a mental illness is factually inaccurate and gets in the way of treatment. What's more, if a young person is already grappling with shame and stigma about an LGBTQ+ identity, further accusations about their mental health are unhelpful.

Anyone experiencing a mental health condition needs compassion, care, and real resources for help. So before you talk with a teenager or their family about any concerns you have, be sure to check your assumptions. Have you come up with a diagnosis as soon as a teenager tells you they're struggling? Do you find yourself dismissing or excusing the signs of depression or anxiety as standard teenage angst? It's easy, and natural, to look for cause-and-effect when a young person shares their heart. And you have the best intentions as you try to solve the problem as quickly and effectively as possible. Yet if your assumptions are left unchecked, you're not going to be the kind of ally you want to be. Quick fixes often feel cheap and uncaring to a teen wrestling with anxiety or depression, as though they're being brushed off or categorized as a victim.

It's also important to understand that, while LGBTQ+ teenagers have higher rates of depression and anxiety, those issues *aren't caused by their queerness.*

The National Mentoring Resource notes that many LGBTQ+ youth are undergoing unique phases of identity development that are "associated with heightened levels of psychological distress—including feelings of isolation, confusion, depression, and questions about belonging and affiliation." They are facing higher likelihood of rejection from family and friends, fear, shame, and discrimination than their straight peers face. And while the causes of anxiety and depression are complicated, we do know that both are caused by chemical imbalances in the brain, which can be exacerbated by stress, loneliness, and fear.

Being queer is not the cause, ever, of anxiety, depression, or any mental illness. If you are looking for a cause, it is the world queer youth must inhabit. The realities of living in a nonaffirming community and having chemical imbalances creating anxiety and depression do compound. Neither of those are caused by a queer identity.

Confront the problem, not a student's authentic identity.

KNOW THE SIGNS AND SYMPTOMS.

Teenagers tend to wear their feelings on their sleeves, but they are also good at covering up emotions or problems they don't want others to know about. So it's crucial that you can recognize the signs and symptoms of depression and anxiety and be ready to offer help even before a teenager tells you they are struggling. Every disorder is different, and each person experiencing a mental health disorder will express it uniquely. Still, there are some resources to help you spot problems before they get worse.

The Mayo Clinic lists the following as symptoms of depression in teens:

EMOTIONAL CHANGES

★ Sadness/crying or frustration/anger even over small matters

★ Feeling hopeless or empty

★ Loss of interest in family, friends, and usual activities

★ Feelings of worthlessness or guilt

★ Fixation on past failures; exaggerated self-blame or self-criticism

★ Extreme sensitivity to rejection or failure, and the need for excessive reassurance

BEHAVIORAL CHANGES

★ Tiredness and loss of energy

★ Insomnia or sleeping too much

★ Changes in appetite; weight loss or gain

★ Alcohol or drug use

★ Social isolation and/or poor school performance

The Mayo Clinic lists the following as symptoms of a general anxiety disorder:

★ Persistent worrying, out of proportion to the impact of events

- Overthinking plans and solutions, and worst-case scenarios
- Inability to set aside or let go of worries
- Inability to relax; restlessness
- Difficulty concentrating
- Fatigue
- Trouble sleeping
- Sweating
- Nausea
- Irritability

These are by no means exhaustive lists. But paying attention to these subtle shifts in behavior can alert you to issues you might not notice otherwise.

Please note: *It's really not your job to diagnose a mental illness.*

But you do have a part to play in getting a student the help they need. Hopefully, you already have a list of trusted mental health professionals and support groups in your community—if not, it's time to start gathering names from other church staff, friends, schools, and databases of professionals in your area. Look for counselors who are accredited by the American Psychological Association (APA), and read counselor reviews on www.healthgrades.com, ADAA's Therapist Directory, or other credible websites. Pay special attention to counselors in your area who are queer or specialize in LGBTQ+ youth work. Remember that not everyone branding themselves as a counselor actually has accreditation or experience in LGBTQ+-specific issues. Put the student's health first, always, in recommending help.

There are also many national resources available to you and your LGBTQ+ students. The Trevor Project is a national organization committed to ending suicide among LGBTQ+ teenagers. They have a 24/7 hotline and lots of solid research on mental health disorders and suicide among LGBTQ+ youth. Even if your queer students haven't talked about suicide or mental health issues, make sure they have this hotline number: 1-866-488-7386 , and the Crisis Text Line: Text "HOME" to 741741.

RECOMMENDATIONS

If you think a teenager is suffering with a mental health condition or if they tell you they are:

+ Don't call them out or speculate publicly about their issues.

+ Don't use scare tactics or start spouting off suicide statistics. Be encouraging. Be loving.

+ Remind them that they are not alone and that they don't need to figure everything out for themselves.

+ Don't immediately share your conversations with the student's parent or guardian. They may not have come out at home, and you could make the situation much worse.

+ Be prepared to recommend specific resources, counselors, and mentors who can provide additional LGBTQ+-specialized support, while assuring your student that you will be supporting them as well.

+ Ask them if they have talked with their parents or guardians about this. Find out what kind of help, if any, they have sought thus far.

+ Be respectful of your student's privacy, but let them know you are obligated to pass on certain information.

+ If the student has expressed thoughts or intentions of self-harm or harming others, you are required to tell their parents or guardians (more about your reporting responsibility on page 166).

+ Emphasize the normalcy of what they are experiencing. Despite being increasingly common in teenagers, depression and anxiety can feel isolating and lonely. Assure your student they are not weird or broken.

★ Make conversations about mental health issues a normal part of your youth ministry. You can do a lot to destigmatize depression and anxiety simply by talking about them as one of the many difficult things people deal with in life.

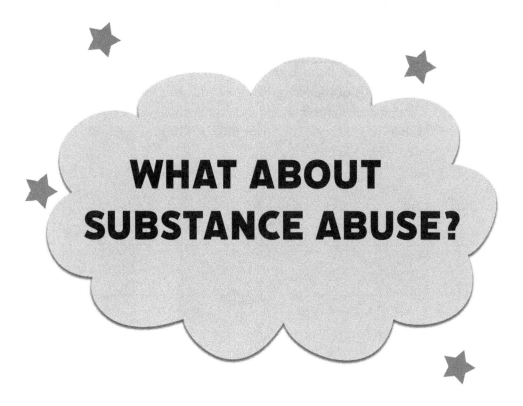

WHAT ABOUT SUBSTANCE ABUSE?

LGBTQ+ youth have higher rates of drug and alcohol use, tobacco use, and other risky behaviors than do their heterosexual peers.[16] Just as with anxiety and depression, risky behaviors do not result from being queer. Drugs, tobacco, and alcohol use are higher among queer teenagers because support systems fail LGBTQ+ youth more often than their straight peers—if there are support systems in place for queer youth at all.

Feelings of loneliness, hopelessness, and worry are all factors that contribute to higher rates of risky behavior. These feelings result from many causes: bullying, harassment, family rejection, social isolation, minority stress, childhood abuse, and more.

THE DATA

Half of all gay, lesbian, and bisexual students surveyed have tried marijuana, compared to 35% of heterosexual students. When it comes to ongoing marijuana use, 30.6% of gay, lesbian, and bisexual students report regular usage, compared to 19.1% of heterosexual students.

Gay, lesbian, and bisexual students were almost two times more likely than heterosexual students to abuse prescription drugs.

 28% of gay, lesbian, and bisexual students had been offered, sold, or given an illegal drug on school property, compared to 18% of heterosexual students.

 More than 20% of gay, lesbian, and bisexual students consumed alcohol for the first time before age 13.

 Binge-drinking rates are almost two times higher among lesbian and bisexual females than heterosexual females.

 LGBTQ+ students were more likely to have ridden with a driver who had been drinking alcohol or using marijuana.

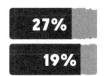 Tobacco use in all forms (cigarette, cigar, smokeless tobacco, or electronic vapor) was higher among gay, lesbian, and bisexual youth (27.2%) than among heterosexual youth (19.2%).

Centers for Disease Control and Prevention

WHAT'S THAT ABOUT?

These stats are not intended to be used as a scare tactic or an indictment on the LGBTQ+ students in your group. And they definitely shouldn't be interpreted as proof that a "gay lifestyle" is one of constant partying and irresponsible behavior. These behaviors are higher among LGBTQ+ students because of two important factors that you can help address.

First, LGBTQ+ students face more environmental, familial, and social pressures than their straight peers do. They are bullied and assaulted more often. They are attacked and discriminated against by family, teachers, peers, and society at large in ways their heterosexual and cisgender peers are not. They face daily stressors that their straight friends do not, and fewer support systems exist to specifically aid LGBTQ+ youth. Like the higher rates of mental health issues, the higher rates of substance abuse and risky behavior among LGBTQ+ students are likely related to the enormous stress they face every day.[17]

Second, LGBTQ+ students receive messages at home, in church, at school, and through popular culture that stigmatize queerness. And LGBTQ+ teenagers are less likely to have positive adult influences in their lives who are willing to talk to them about their sexual orientation and gender identity, teach them how to navigate through the straight world, and help protect them from harmful situations.[18]

Teachers, leaders, and, yes, the church have all failed to protect and instruct LGBTQ+ teenagers on the specific risks of being a young queer person today. It should come as no surprise then that our LGBTQ+ kids are turning to the same risky behaviors as their peers, but in higher numbers.

You might be the only positive, protective voice in a young LGBTQ+ person's life. Talk openly about the risks they face and the potentially harmful situations they might encounter. Invite open discussion about drug and alcohol use, along with conversations about mental health, stress, and peer pressure. Create a judgment-free zone that focuses on listening to your queer students rather than reading a list of the ways drug use will ruin their lives.

Never use fear as a motivator. Your goal is to empower, not to invoke shame or guilt.

A FINAL THOUGHT

If one of your students does tell you they are using drugs or alcohol or participating in other risky behaviors, it might be a good idea to tell their parents. But it also might be a very bad idea.

If loving and affirming LGBTQ+ youth is the aim of your work with queer teens (and it absolutely should be), remember that lots of parents do not agree. Many families, especially religious families, are not affirming. Telling them their kid is using drugs or participating in risky behavior may lead to that kid being outted, and that in turn may only increase the behaviors you're trying to stop.

You'll have to use your own discernment and discretion on this, but always put the well-being of your student first.

IS IT EVER OKAY TO RECOMMEND CONVERSION THERAPY?

No. Never. Ever. *Ever.*

Yes, we have strong opinions about this. Here's why:

Conversion therapy, also known as reparative therapy, is any practice aimed at intentionally changing someone's sexual orientation or gender identity. These practices have been in use in various forms since the 1890s and are still common today.[19]

Methods of conversion therapy have differed through the years. Talk therapy and pray-the-gay-away are currently among the most popular practices. Historically, conversion therapy employed some truly terrifying methods, such as aversion therapy, in an attempt to change a person's orientation or identity. Aversion therapy involves using nausea, vomiting, electric shocks, or other forms of self-inflicted pain as a punishment for arousal by same-sex erotic thoughts or images. This type of therapy has been condemned by mental health professionals.[20]

It's impossible to know just what kinds of conversion therapy are still in use, or just how common it is.

What we do know is this:

- ★ Nearly 700,000 LGBTQ+ adults in the United States have undergone conversion therapy at some point in their lives.

- ★ About half of these people received conversion therapy as teenagers.

- ★ An estimated 57,000 teenagers (ages 13–17) across the US will receive conversion therapy in a religious or spiritual context before they are 18.
(Williams Institute)

DOES CONVERSION THERAPY WORK?

No.

Conversion therapy is rooted in the assumption that homosexuality is a mental illness or abnormality, which the American Psychological Association (APA) rejected in 1973. All peer-reviewed clinical research and literature demonstrate that same-sex attraction is a normal, natural variation of human sexuality. To this day, no credible scientific research has been able to prove that conversion therapy can change someone's gender identity or sexual orientation.

Not only is conversion therapy not effective; it is dangerous. Nearly every medical and mental health organization has discredited and denounced conversion therapy because of its harmful effects. The APA warns, "The potential risks of reparative therapy are great, including depression, anxiety, and self-destructive behavior, since therapist alignment with societal prejudices against homosexuality may reinforce self-hatred already experienced by the patient."

The American Academy of Child and Adolescent Psychiatry cautions against therapeutic efforts to change a minor's orientation, saying these efforts may "encourage family rejection and undermine self-esteem, connectedness, and caring, important protective factors against suicidal ideation and attempts."

PERILS OF CONVERSION THERAPY:

 Teenagers who had undergone conversion therapy or experienced someone trying to force them to change their orientation or identity were more than twice as likely to attempt suicide as those who had not.

 Of the LGBTQ+ teenagers who have attempted suicide, 42% have undergone conversion therapy.

 57% of transgender and nonbinary teenagers who have undergone conversion therapy report a suicide attempt in the last year.

The Trevor Project

Read those again. These are not just numbers. These are actual young lives that ended, or very nearly ended, because of conversion therapy.

Despite these shocking numbers, conversion therapy is still legal in most states. As of this publication, nineteen states, along with Washington, DC, and Puerto Rico, had banned conversion therapy. Certain municipalities in other states have banned it as well, even while the state as a whole still has not done so.

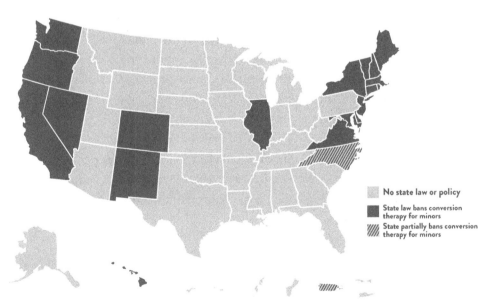

No state law or policy

State law bans conversion therapy for minors

State partially bans conversion therapy for minors

Check to see what your state's legislation on conversion therapy is at www.lgbtmap.org/equality-maps/conversion_therapy.

CONVERSION THERAPY IN THE CHURCH

Even in states that ban conversion therapy, these laws don't apply to religious or spiritual leaders who advise changing sexual orientation and gender identity through their pastoral care and teaching. This leaves thousands of LGBTQ+ teenagers vulnerable to the harmful effects of conversion therapy tactics. Look into your church's and denomination's policies on using conversion therapy. If your church allows or even encourages conversion therapy—any suggestion of or pressure to "change" one's sexual orientation or gender identity is conversion therapy—please use the information in this section to warn of the dangers of conversion therapy. It's a failed and harmful practice, and it has to stop.

Regardless of where your church stands theologically regarding LGBTQ+ people, you have a right and responsibility to protect young people from a practice that causes psychological, emotional, and physical harm. If your church has no declared stance on conversion therapy, consider adopting an anti–conversion therapy policy. Having clear language in place about this practice creates a safe space for teenagers and families, as well as safeguarding you from potential issues and liability surrounding this issue.

A FINAL THOUGHT

We know we've just unloaded a lot of startling facts and figures on you. Yet ultimately, we want to emphasize the experience of an LGBTQ+ child or teenager who has undergone or may undergo conversion therapy. They are rejected by family and faith communities. They are told that they are an anomaly, that their desires make them inherently invaluable and disgusting. They are told they must be fixed. They are subjected to psychologically unhealthy practices that lead to depression, anxiety, and possibly suicide.

We'll say it again. Regardless of where you and your church stand on homosexuality, this type of treatment of young people is not true to the heart of our Creator. This should not be how we love.

Mia, 21:

Not only does [the country I come from] have laws against queer people and queer relationships, but most of the churches in my hometown also think that it is a mental health issue. Although it wasn't preferable, I resorted to consulting church-related resources to reach out to talk about what I was experiencing. Every session was the same . . .

"Love the sinner but hate the sin."

"They need love and help from us to get better."

"There have been many who were saved because of the love of Christ. Now they're in happy, loving, normal relationships that do not go against God's word."

For the longest time I've internalized these words, to the point that I only knew how to hate that part of myself because it was how I showed that I "loved" God. It takes a while to heal from thinking that there is something wrong with how you love. I still experience this today from other pastors and leaders in my life. Sometimes, it helps to break out of the environment you're used to in order to have a breakthrough. It happened for me when I decided to reach out to organizations, friends, and families that open doors to the LGBTQ+ community. Reaching out to those who want to make an effort to understand you better and support you for that can make a huge difference in your life. You don't need any saving. You don't need to "get better."

UNDERSTANDING THE STATISTICS ON LGBTQ+ SUICIDE

Suicide is a harsh reality for today's youth. The Centers for Disease Control and Prevention reported that between 2007 and 2017, the rate of teenage suicide increased 56 percent. Even if a teenager hasn't been suicidal themselves, the odds are strong that they know someone who has been, or who has died by suicide. You probably do too. Knowing the stats on suicide will help you recognize when someone is struggling, equip you with a healthy response, and enable you to have more effective conversations about this difficult subject with young people and your faith community.

Suicide is the second-leading cause of death among teenagers. According to a study done by the Trevor Project, LGBTQ+ youth are four times more likely than their non-LGBTQ+ peers to consider, make a plan for, and attempt suicide. These numbers from a 2019 survey are sobering:

1.8 MILLION **13–24 YEARS OLD**

Over 1.8 million LGBTQ+ people ages 13–24 consider suicide each year.

ATTEMPTED | **CONSIDERED**

Almost half of LGBTQ+ youth 13–17 have considered suicide. More than 25% of LGBTQ+ youth have attempted suicide.

LGB students were three and a half times more likely to consider suicide than their heterosexual peers (47.7% vs. 13.3%).

LGB

QUESTIONING

38% of LGB students and 25.6% of questioning students had made a plan about how they would attempt suicide.

ATTEMPTED | **CONSIDERED**

Over half of transgender and nonbinary youth have seriously considered suicide and 29% had attempted it.

The Trevor Project

And perhaps the most alarming for church leaders:

LGBTQ+ youth who said that religion was "very important" to them were 38% more likely to attempt suicide.
American Journal of Preventive Medicine

That last one should sting. LGBTQ+ teenagers who value religion are more likely to attempt suicide than those who don't. Without knowing the circumstances of these individuals, we can't speak to why that's the case. But whether a teenager is part of an open and affirming family and church or not, they still hear and experience bigotry in the name of religion on a regular basis. Clearly, that takes a terrible toll.

All of us, in every single church, have to address the ways in which the larger Christian church, and our individual congregations, are making life more unbearable for queer kids. We have to do better.

The causes of suicide are complex and unique to each person. And there's no single fix to ending suicide. However, it's possible to point to some factors that increase the likelihood of a queer teen considering or attempting suicide:

+ Family rejection
+ Conversion therapy
+ Experiencing physical harm or bullying
+ Experiencing discrimination based on their identity or orientation
+ Lack of supportive adults in their life
+ Placing high importance on religion

TALKING ABOUT SUICIDE

First, and very, very importantly: many LGBTQ+ teenagers are happy and well-adjusted in their sexual orientation and identity. It's crucial not to make assumptions about queer teens regarding their mental and emotional health. Nevertheless, it's important to be aware of, and take seriously, a young person's attitude, behavior, and language concerning suicide.

Early warning signs of suicide:[21]

TALK ABOUT:

* Killing themselves (jokingly or not)
* Feeling hopeless
* Having no reason to live
* Being a burden
* Feeling trapped
* Unbearable pain

BEHAVIORS:

* Increased use of drugs or alcohol
* Withdrawing from activities
* Isolating from family and friends
* Sleeping too much or too little

- ★ Visiting or calling people to say goodbye
- ★ Giving away possessions
- ★ Fatigue

MOODS:
- ★ Depression
- ★ Anxiety
- ★ Loss of interest
- ★ Irritability
- ★ Shame and humiliation
- ★ Anger
- ★ Relief

If you notice any of these signs, meet with the individual privately and ask some questions. This helps determine the level of immediate danger, as well as offering immediate support. Here are a few suggestions of what to ask (see full list in Appendix 206):[22]

- ★ How are you coping with what's been happening in your life?
- ★ Are you thinking about dying? Hurting yourself? Killing yourself?
- ★ Have you thought about how or when you'd do it?
- ★ Do you have access to weapons or things that can be used to harm yourself?
- ★ Have you talked to anyone about this?

These questions may seem counterintuitive, as they encourage a person to seriously confront the idea of suicide. But they aren't going to push someone more quickly into self-destructive behavior. Instead, asking questions creates a safe space for the young person to discuss their feelings and confront the reality of their ideas. Sometimes verbally admitting, "Yes, I am thinking about trying, or planning, to end my life" can help a teenager admit the depth of their pain and open up to finding help.

Obviously, you need to know and adhere to your church's policy on reporting thoughts or attempts of suicide and self-harm. If your church doesn't have a written response for leaders, enact one immediately. Look up "The Role of Faith Communities in Preventing Suicide" from the Suicide Prevention Resource Center for a good starting place.

REVERSING THE STATISTICS

We want to end with some of the most uplifting research we have found about LGBTQ+ teenagers and suicide. In 2018, The Trevor Project found that having just one accepting adult in their life reduced a queer teenager's likelihood of a suicide attempt by 40 percent.[23] While having accepting parents is one of the biggest factors, this study revealed that any accepting adult has the ability to reduce a queer teenager's odds of attempting suicide.

You can be that one accepting adult. In fact, it's possible you are the only adult a young queer person has come out to. Your love and acceptance can quite literally save lives. This is not to say that you are solely in charge of a young person's decisions or that any suicide attempt is your fault. But be encouraged that you have the power to change a young person's decision to end their life. You absolutely have the ability, but you also have the responsibility to be source of grace, care, and belonging for a queer teenager.

Zoe, 28:

> I was at a friend's house, and she showed me that she would cut herself with a razor blade. I winced at the thought. I was super squeamish and could never think of doing that. However, a few days later, I started scratching my upper thigh with a broken piece of plastic and realized it did bring some form of distraction. The pain distracted me from all of the feelings and confusion. So, after doing that for a while, I switched to scissors, and after a year, a knife. It became the only way that I could feel anything after becoming so numb to the outside world. When I grew into adulthood, it just got worse. I didn't have anyone to talk to, no adult to tell me that who I am was okay, and that I was loved no matter what my sexuality is.

After a few falls to rock bottom, I went begrudgingly back to the church. What I found was nothing short of a miracle. I was free to worship again, knowing what I know now. I found people I could talk to about my woes and lift the anxiety. I found others just like me. So even though the depression is still there, it's a lot less stressful nowadays. The most helpful thing was finding my creative outlet in art and filmmaking and exercising. Getting some bench presses in really gets out all the bad energy from your system. I exercise every other day, hang out with friends, play games, go out for the occasional drink. And most importantly, I still go to church to worship as often as I can.

HOW DO I KNOW THEY AREN'T JUST LOOKING FOR ATTENTION?

Sometimes people think of coming out as queer as *taking on* an LGBTQ+ identity, rather than revealing one. After a teenager comes out, parents and church leaders might speculate that the student isn't *really* queer, but rather, that they're trying to get noticed or be rebellious or be quirky. Maybe you've heard other adults say things like, "Everyone thinks they're gay these days," or "They're just being dramatic."

In our individualistic culture, it's easy to label anyone expressing emotion or asking for support as needy or burdensome. But showing emotion and wanting attention do not equal weakness or selfishness. Nor are they legitimate excuses to ignore or invalidate what a teenager is telling you with their words or actions.

Yes, the emotions of teenagers tend to be intense and can fluctuate widely from one moment to the next. But as you know, these emotions are spurred by the many physical, mental, and sociological changes occurring in a young person's life during puberty and throughout adolescence. From hormones to test anxiety to legitimately stressful decisions (like, you know, life after graduation), teenagers are immersed in emotionally charged situations.

These internal and external factors will affect how a teenager speaks, thinks, and tells their story. But they do not make what they have to say any less real or valid. And they don't make a student's journey of self-discovery less important. A teenager expressing emotion or talking through any kind of difficult topic should never be brushed aside.

In the same way, a young person who identifies as LGBTQ+ should never be viewed as inauthentic or disingenuous simply because of the emotion involved. They are not riding an impulse or trying to garner attention from their peers. Many young people agonize over the decision to come out. They have weighed the factors of rejection, discrimination, and invalidation. They are likely facing familial, peer, or religious disapproval.

This is certainly not the kind of attention they are seeking by coming out.

WHAT'S WRONG WITH LOOKING FOR A LITTLE ATTENTION?

There's very (*very*) little research to suggest that young people come out purely for attention. As someone who knows and cares about teenagers, you understand that young people are easily dismissed by many of the adults in their lives.

You can flip the script and be an adult who understands that looking for attention is a perfectly reasonable human longing. Wanting other people to look at, listen to, and care about you isn't a problem. It's normal to want to be seen. So if an LGBTQ+ student in your group is "seeking attention," give it to them! Some—if not most—of the attention they will receive for coming out will be negative and, at times, abusive. So give them loving, affirming, compassionate attention instead.

RECOMMENDATIONS

The risk of ignoring or not believing a student who is coming out far outweighs whatever concerns you or other adults might have about indulging their perceived need for attention. Without support during this crucial process, a student's isolation and loneliness can increase, and negative behaviors can be established.

You won't "turn off" their process of self-discovery by ignoring it. Instead, they're likely to look elsewhere for acceptance and information. Not only will you lose their trust, but you'll lose the opportunity to guide them toward resources and people who will help them make good decisions about their future.

Believe what your LGBTQ+ students tell you about themselves as they express and explore their identity. It's a tremendous privilege to accompany them and participate in an important, life-changing process and become a trusted resource and supporter through your curiosity, empathy, and acceptance.

A FINAL THOUGHT

We are all on a journey of self-discovery. While this process is certainly not limited to adolescence, these tender years are crucial for a young queer person. Show them that there is freedom to learn, to flounder, to make mistakes. If a young person takes this journey of self-discovery in a safe space, they are being set up for an emotionally healthy, confident life.

Anthoni, 28:

> I got this response ["You're doing this for attention"] from a church counselor when I was thirteen. I'd been so nervous to say I liked girls out loud that I had to lean my head back against the wall because I thought I was going to pass out. She promptly assured me I was probably just looking for a sense of identity like anyone my age. She suggested that thinking I was gay because I liked girls was like someone who assumes they have a brain tumor every time they get a headache. Basically, I was overreacting. She said all this with such misguided warmth and reassurance that I believed her.
>
> That conversation was devastating, and I would beg anyone in a position of influence not to let this be your knee-jerk reaction. If someone comes to you with this, it probably took them months or years to get to that conclusion and took a lot of courage to decide on sharing their feelings in a world that has a lot of opinions about

those feelings. They simply know themselves, feel proud of who they are, and want to let people know. I wish I had been so confident as a teen. If they wanted to be loud and proud about their Christian identity, or any other major part of themselves, it's unlikely anyone would question their sincerity.

Any type of attention you might get from being queer, especially as someone in a faith community, is hardly desirable. I was about fourteen when Massachusetts became the first state to legalize same-sex marriage. I was very aware of my preference for girls by then, and I heard the vicious national response all around me. I—a kid who loved baking, history books, visiting my grandpa, and volunteering with friends—heard myself put in the same category as murderers and people who have sex with dogs, heard that I was ruining families, that God wouldn't be able to stand having someone like me around him in Heaven. In Sunday school, I heard all about how LGBTQ+ people were "too loud," "too obnoxious," "attention whores," too everything.

I can't imagine why anyone would ever come out for attention if this was the kind of attention they were going to get.

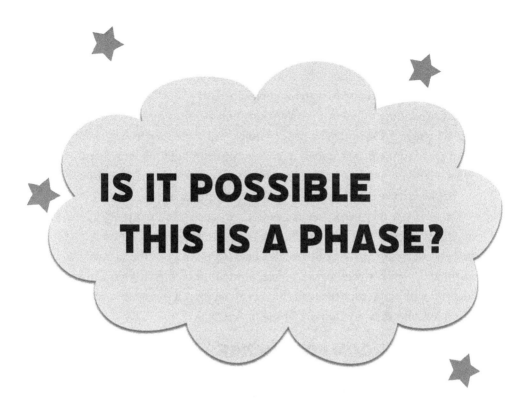

IS IT POSSIBLE THIS IS A PHASE?

People go through all kinds of phases. Teenagers in particular are rapidly moving through various stages of adolescent development. The young people at your church may look, sound, and act different from week to week. They'll be trying new things, exploring their growing independence, and experimenting with new hobbies, interests, clubs, and social groups. It's a lot to keep up with.

You might find yourself wondering, given the many stages they're going through, if a queer kid's identity might just be one phase among many. It might feel like a reasonable, innocent question that you or others are asking. However, this kind of speculation can be difficult for a young person to hear and could jeopardize your role as a trusted, caring adult.

TRUST LGBTQ+ PEOPLE

If you imply, wonder, question, or state that this might be a phase, you're communicating that you don't fully believe what they're telling you. It suggests that you think being queer is easy, something that can be chosen. That queerness makes someone popular, and can be rejected or "grown out of" when one gets older.

Don't kid yourself about the consequences of coming out. It's tough.

There are short- and long-term perspectives at play when you consider how you're going to interact with a young person who comes out. Coming out is a process. One that can happen quickly or can take decades. If, for example, a young person comes out as gay while in high school but ten years later comes out as transgender, it doesn't necessarily mean their high school identity was a phase. It's all part of a long journey.

Similarly, if they come out as gay in high school, and ten years later they declare that they are bisexual or pansexual or just refuse to be labeled, again, no part of that is a phase. It's all part of the process. Ultimately, neither you nor your queer student knows what their future identity will be. Accept them for who they say they are now, and accept them for who they say they are in the future.

CREATING ROOM FOR CHANGE

People who work with teenagers—teachers, counselors, coaches, and youth ministers—understand better than anyone how to roll with the changes experienced by young people. As their bodies, brains, and identities change, so too does your approach to ministry. Make sure you're creating physical, emotional, and spiritual room for young people to be themselves as fully as possible when they're at church and with your group.

You can also help the families of LGBTQ+ youth through their teenager's coming-out process. Get permission from your student to talk with their parents about the change their family is experiencing. Listen to the parents' concerns or questions about what this new identity will mean for their family, friends, and larger community. Above all else, encourage them to love and support their child, even if that means shielding their teenager from some of the relational fallout that might be coming their way.

PHASE CAN BECOME A PATHWAY TO CONVERSION THERAPY

Be on the lookout for words or phrases that suggest parents or family members aren't accepting their teenager's identity. For example, if parents are using "phase" language it could be a sign that they would consider conversion therapy when that phase does not come to an end.

Speak kindly, but firmly, to debunk the idea that this is a phase. If conversion therapy comes up, stress that this is not a helpful option and can create lasting, damaging effects to their teenager. Indicate that what might look like a phase to parents or other family members could be something the teenager has been considering for a long time.

A FINAL THOUGHT

Believing a young person doesn't make you gullible or stupid; it makes you compassionate. The reality is, we all go through stages and phases of identity as we figure out who we are and how we want to live in the world. The fact that we change and shift as we get older doesn't negate the person we were before. It's all part of the same story. So don't worry about whether or not the labels a student uses for themselves today are the same ones they use next week or next year.

Just believe them. They know who they are better than you do. Better than anyone. Your example of love and acceptance will sustain your queer student, their family, and your church community throughout all phases, stages, and changes.

Claire, 21:

> I know that sometimes people go through phases. There's an "emo" phase, there's a "goth" phase, and I'm vaguely certain that every university student goes through a "smoothies for breakfast" phase (mine was during my first year). The problem with calling something a "phase" is how negative its connotations are. There's nothing wrong with going through a "phase," even, and especially, when it comes to your identity. There's nothing wrong with learning new ways to address and interpret what you feel. So even if it is a "phase," it will never be "just" a phase. Mine shaped who I am today. I'm still here, I'm still Queer. There's nothing wrong with being transgender or bisexual or gay or genderqueer or asexual or having any Queer identity. Even if it is a phase, that's perfectly fine. You're still valid, loved, and important.

Faith, 23:

Even though I grew up in a very queer-affirming household and congregation, it took me a long time to come to terms with my various queer identities, in part because I didn't have the vocabulary for all the parts of myself for a long time after I began to feel my identity stirring within me. Today, I identify as asexual, biromantic, and nonbinary, but it has been a long journey to get here. While I had inklings of being asexual and biromantic starting in early adolescence, identifying as nonbinary came as a surprise. Looking back, I do remember feeling like "one of the guys" sometimes as a child, like when I was at chess club or on the science team, and other times feeling like a girl, like when I got dressed up for church. But it took until midway through college to realize that this was a pattern and I might want a word for it, and another year and a half after that to get up the courage to start coming out as nonbinary. I still haven't figured out pronouns. I've learned that it's okay for figuring things out to take a while.

HOW SHOULD I HANDLE QUESTIONS ABOUT SEX?

Teenagers think and talk about sex. A lot. If they're talking about sex at church with peers and trusted adults, then congratulations! That means you're seen as a safe, trustworthy resource for tough, potentially awkward conversations. It's an honor to be trusted with these questions. Clearly, you're doing this right.

Our sexuality is an important part of our humanity and the way God made us, and not just because of procreation. Sex is an intimate expression of love between partners. It's beautiful. It's sacred. And it should be discussed through the lens of faith.

Even when you've been having healthy conversations with teenagers about sex, relationships, and faith for years, you might feel a little out of your depth when it comes to having these conversations with queer teenagers. Unless you're LGBTQ+ yourself, it's likely you don't have a lot of good information about the dating and sex lives of queer people. That can leave you feeling ill-equipped to help LGBTQ+ students in your group get good information and make good decisions.

QUEERING THE "SEX TALK"

The good news is that, when it comes to talking about sex and relationships with LGBTQ+ teenagers, your approach doesn't need to be all that different from the way you talk with straight and cis teenagers. So think about how you give your "sex talk," the ways you talk about dating or marriage or family life. Consider the assumptions built into any materials you use, including talks you've put together yourself.

* Are you promoting an exclusively heteronormative view of dating? Don't.

* Do you assume teenagers cannot be open about their dating lives? Stop.

* Does your language assume a binary understanding of desire, hormones, and romance? Change it.

* Does anything you say encourage a "purity" mindset that builds shame into a teenager's understanding of their body and their sexual desires? Cut it immediately.

* Even your straight students will benefit from eliminating language that tells them boys only want one thing and girls are objects to be protected from male desire.

Even making these routine changes will begin to establish your role as an inclusive and affirming resource for all of your students when it comes to discussions of sexuality and gender.

BUT WHAT ABOUT ACTUAL LGBTQ+ SEX?

LGBTQ+ teenagers receive very little information about queer sexuality and gender identities from the adults in their lives. Even schools that have some curricula generally cover a broad range of LGBTQ+ topics in a short time and without much detail. If teens aren't out—or even if they are—their (presumably) straight parents might not have much to offer either.

And this is a problem when it comes to queer sex, because, honestly, a lot of young people don't know how to have queer sex. Literally. And this lack of knowledge can be dangerous. Most of their knowledge about sex likely comes from the internet, which can be, as with all things, wonderfully useful or very, very unhelpful.

This creates a vacuum, but it's also an opportunity. You can become a reliable, safe, honest resource for LGBTQ+ teenager talks to about sex and gender.

Of course, that also means knowing a thing or two about queer sexuality and gender. We don't have the space here to teach you the details of queer sex, but we can direct you toward some invaluable resources.

* The curriculum *Our Whole Lives* is an excellent sexual education course for teenagers both queer and not.

* Online resources, like Scarleteen, provide frank and honest answers to LGBTQ+ sex and gender questions. There are just some topics you won't (and shouldn't) be comfortable talking about with teenagers. Send them to Scarleteen, or other sources that have deep-dive content for LGBTQ+ young people.

* See our appendix titled "Additional Resources" on page 190.

Please know your own limits and comfort level. Sex questions need to be answered with accurate, affirming, sex-positive information. Whether it comes from you or you provide direction on how to find it doesn't really matter in the end.

MORE THAN JUST SEX

Faith-based sex education is becoming more robust, moving away from purity culture and shame-based conversations. It is no longer relevant or instructive for adult leaders to tell young people what to do with their bodies, to draw lines around behavior, or to lead conversations like "How far is too far?" or "What technically counts as sex?" Today, useful faith-based conversations are about students' bodies, their spirituality, and their partners.

As you talk with your students—LBTGQ+ and straight/cis alike—help them consider who they want to be and the kinds of relationships they want to have. Give them tools to talk openly with their partners about what they do and don't like, what they are and aren't willing to do. Talk about consent and autonomy. Remind them that if they can't talk about sex and consent and boundaries with their partner, they're probably not ready for sex. Encourage young people to be thoughtful and cautious, but avoid anything that looks or sounds like shame-based sex ed.

RECOMMENDATIONS

When an LGBTQ+ teenager comes to you with questions about sex, try to answer the questions they're really asking. Resist the impulse to make one person's question into a lengthy sermon. Avoid putting your story into theirs or making assumptions about their future. Convey the values taught by your church with care and grace. Give them a framework for making their best decisions. Help them understand the dangers and pleasures of being a sexual being.

If you have no idea what to say, that's okay too. If you're not LGBTQ+, it's very reasonable that you don't know the ins and outs of queer sex. Practice your reaction face and saying "I don't know" without judgment. Help your student find the resources and information they need. Walk together in the quest for knowledge and understanding. If you're shocked or grossed out, keep it to yourself. If you need to opt out of certain topics, be honest about that, and refer them to another adult who might have a different level of comfort for these discussions.

And really, it's okay that you don't know everything. You are the trusted adult in the room, but your student is the expert on their sexuality. Trust them to take your guidance to heart and apply it to their own lives.

A FINAL THOUGHT

It is possible to be open about the goodness of sex and still speak up about the risks of sexual activity. Listen for young people who describe problems, dangers, or unsafe situations. Reach out to a counselor or LGBTQ+ center if you need to. Many young people have learned about the mechanics of sex, the principles of conception, and sexually transmitted infections in school health classes. But these classes are aimed at heterosexual scenarios. For example, young gay men often don't use condoms because they're taught that condoms are about avoiding pregnancy and STIs during vaginal sex (for what it's worth: condoms, always, everyone!).

Your LGBTQ+ students will face issues that simply do not get covered in school or at home. It's a guarantee. You'll need to keep your radar tuned in to any iffy situations they might tell you about. Your overriding message is about the holistic physical and emotional safety of every student in your care.

WHAT ABOUT PORN?

Let's be honest. Teenagers look at pornography. Fifty-seven percent of teens seek out pornography once a month, with the average first exposure to porn coming at age twelve.[24] So it's pretty much a certainty that some of the students in your group have been exposed to explicit photos or videos involving sex.

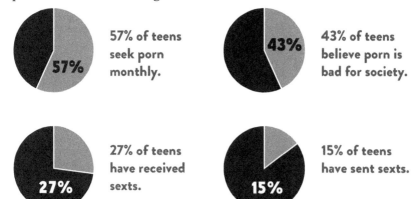

57% of teens seek porn monthly.

43% of teens believe porn is bad for society.

27% of teens have received sexts.

15% of teens have sent sexts.

Covenant Eyes

The pervasiveness of web-enabled mobile devices, coupled with millions of free porn websites, means teenagers don't have to work very hard to access the world of pornography. Young people in particular are curious about their bodies. Surges in hormone levels are making them more interested in physical contact and sexual gratification. And more and more, kids are talking with each other about sex and even sending sexually explicit pictures and videos to each other. With all of this heightened exposure to sexual content, it's important for you to know how to enter the conversation in appropriate ways.

THE BOTTOM LINE

Some of this might seem obvious to you, but we think it's important to reiterate it so you have really clear boundaries of where you can and can't go. It's illegal for an adult to show porn to minors, even for instructional or cautionary purposes. It is illegal to share nude or sexual images of an underage person. Nude selfies are not art. They're child pornography, which is a sexual offense. Furthermore, never speak about your personal experience with pornography.

QUEER YOUTH AND PORN

All teenagers who watch porn do it because they're curious or looking for gratification. That's true of queer and straight youth. But some LGBTQ+ teenagers have a different relationship to porn than their straight or cis peers. For them, porn is about curiosity, yes, but it's also about exploration and education. Many teenagers have never heard or seen *anything* about queer sex. It's not normalized in popular culture. They don't see simulated queer sex in movies or have diagrams in their sex ed books. Sexual interaction, just like romantic relationships, are just not modeled for them in culture.

So they often look to other sources of media, like porn, for information about intimacy between queer people. Sure, maybe they'd rather read a book or watch a movie on the subject, but the guilt, shame, or fear of being queer (or even exploring the idea of querness) could make a trip to the library for such a book or streaming a movie on Netflix impossible. Porn, on the other hand, is easy to find, free, and anonymous.

When speaking about porn with queer teenagers, avoid shaming their instinct to seek it out, and don't assume you know why they're looking for it. Trying to make them feel guilty about watching porn won't keep them from looking at porn; it'll just mean they'll be less likely to trust you with their questions or concerns about sex.

Instead, consider that your job is to help students understand and process their sexuality, even as they're using pornography as part of that process.

THE PROBLEMS OF PORN

We are not suggesting you establish a free-wheeling, pro-porn approach (though this is a good time to examine your own relationship to pornography, if you have one). Porn is difficult to make sense of, and we don't think it's good for teens for lots of reasons. Here are a few:

★ It's not real. It's a fantasy that should not be reenacted.

★ The pornography industry is filled with oppression, harm, and trafficking.

★ The staging of porn scenes is often misogynistic, racist, violent, and unconcerned with mutual pleasure.

★ There are questionable consent issues related to the people having sex in porn.

★ The sex shown in pornography isn't representative of safe, real, or intimate sex between people who love and trust each other.

★ Porn reinforces terrible body messages for people of all genders and identities.

This list could go on for a very long time. In short, porn is problematic in many ways. It's like fast food: short-term satisfaction with long-term damage.

If you discover that an LGBTQ+ teenager is watching porn, your first responsibility is to determine if there are any safety issues, such as grooming or coercion. If you don't believe their safety is a factor, consider your discovery to be confidential information. Talk with your student and share your concerns with them. Whatever you do, do not out their use of queer pornography to their family. Telling parents that their child is looking at queer porn is tantamount to outing them.

Make sure you know what your church teaches about porn, and be consistent with how you speak about it with your queer and nonqueer students. Provide information, facts, and alternatives like ethically sourced sexual education resources.

As with most potentially problematic issues in your group, it will save you a lot of trouble to have a clear policy about online behavior when students are in the church or participating in a youth group activity. In the same way you have rules around weapons, tobacco, and alcohol use at church functions, create and state your clear expectations about watching and sharing porn—including sexting and sharing explicit images—with your group.

A FINAL THOUGHT

Porn is not sex education. It might be fun to watch. It could even be helpful and informative. But it's not something to treat as anything other than what it is. Pornography.

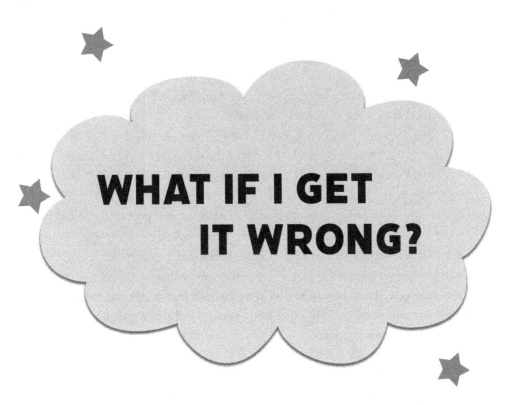

WHAT IF I GET IT WRONG?

There are a lot of opportunities to say the wrong thing when talking to or about your LGBTQ+ students. You'll say something insensitive (such as using the wrong name). You'll just let the little things slide (like continuing to use binary gender language). You'll misread a signal from a teen too afraid to be direct. You'll do something. It just happens. To everyone.

So just accept it: in this process of learning and interacting with LGBTQ+ teenagers, you're going to get it wrong sometimes.

NOW WHAT?

In that horrible moment of realization, it's easy to get defensive or tumble into shame and guilt. Both responses often lead to making excuses for your actions (or inactions) or just hoping no one noticed. But as soon as we fall into this way of thinking, we've immediately made the situation all about us. We've focused on our actions and our reputation instead of the feelings of the young person involved. How you respond after making a mistake should be entirely focused on ensuring the safety, security, and reaffirmation of the teenager.

Here's how to do that:

- Acknowledge your mistake, regardless of whether it was intentional or unintentional.

- Name your specific action and acknowledge why it's problematic. For example, "I realize I used your former name and I know that's hurtful. I'm sorry."

- Allow them a chance—in private—to express how your actions affected them. They might not want to talk about it, but give them room in your apology to tell you what they're feeling.

- Don't be defensive or shift the blame. Using phrases like "It's going to take me a while to get used to this" or "You have to expect mistakes" puts the blame for your actions on a young person's identity or orientation. An LGBTQ+ person isn't responsible for other people's insensitivity.

- Don't say you'll try to do better; just do better. Yes, it takes time to get used to a new name or new pronouns; it takes practice to change your understanding of and language around sexuality and gender. But that's your work to do. And when you care about someone, you do the work necessary to see them as they see themselves. That's an act of love.

You can also take steps to avoid mistakenly hurting a queer young person:

- Educate yourself about *why* it's important to use the names and pronouns of LGBTQ+ people. It's a big deal to change these things, and asking others to use them indicates a major milestone in a person's life.

- Practice using the names or pronouns, not just to the young person's face, but anytime you are speaking, thinking, or praying about them. If you only use the correct language to the person, you're not affirming them; you're just placating them.

★ Learn to recognize microaggressions and the ways they affect an LGBTQ+ person. Avoid stereotypes and assumptions about a person's sexuality, gender, or orientation. Pay attention to the ways your volunteers and other students treat and talk to your LGBTQ+ student, and make sure they are being kind and compassionate in their interactions as well.

★ Remember that discomfort is growth. Learn from the situation; don't walk away or ignore it.

THE LITTLE THINGS

Getting the big picture of how to treat LGBTQ+ teenagers with dignity is crucial, and it's where we all start. But avoid patting yourself on the back for being inclusive. When that happens, it's easy to start letting the little things slide.

If you're part of an open and affirming church, that's wonderful, but it does not mean your work is done. Many welcoming Christian communities are still full of microaggressions.

> **microaggression:** *noun*
>
> A statement, action, or incident regarded as an instance of indirect, subtle, or unintentional discrimination or prejudice against members of a marginalized group
>
> *(Oxford)*

Be aware of microaggressions you might be committing. The presence of microaggressions often gets overlooked because churches think that they've "already done the work." But repeated use of language that is exclusive or heteronormative is enough to send many queer youth looking for a new faith community. This is why it's so crucial not only to grow in your own behavior but to advocate for your queer teenagers throughout your church.

RECOMMENDATIONS

* If you're still in the moment when you realize you've made a mistake, apologize. Don't go overboard explaining yourself or your actions. Instead, transition to what you learned and what you want to do differently.

* If you're called out by an LGBTQ+ youth for a mistake or microaggression you didn't realize you did, listen. Don't be defensive or respond with excuses. By being teachable and repentant, you're not only deepening a young person's trust; you're modeling a mature response and teachable spirit to the rest of your group, staff, volunteers, and even parents.

* If you don't know what to do differently next time, ask. Chances are, if you don't know the right response, the young person involved does. Ask them, "How would you have liked me to respond? What can I do differently next time?"

* If you participated in a larger system of oppression (intentionally or by accident), acknowledge the harm and talk about it out loud. Then move to what you want to do about it. The goal of apologizing is not to release yourself from any blame, but to restore relationships. Take time to listen to the pain these systems have caused. Talk about what can be changed, first one-on-one with the affected person, then with the larger group if that's appropriate. Oppressive systems are brought down by intentional action, not passive avoidance of the issues.

* Be an advocate for your LGBTQ+ students. Talk to your pastoral team, volunteers, adult groups, etc. about how to make your entire community more welcoming and affirming.

A FINAL THOUGHT

Mistakes don't make you an unloving, unsupportive person. Mistakes are opportunities to learn and grow. They're chances for you to model a grace-filled and humble response. Even through your mistakes, you have an opportunity to lead your congregation toward reconciliation as well as to create a safe space built on trust.

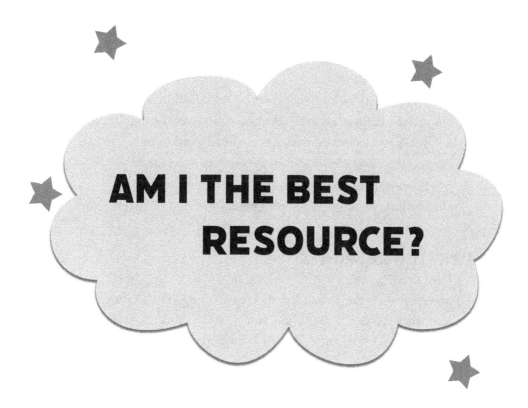

AM I THE BEST RESOURCE?

We know the immense pressure church leaders face. You're in a position of authority, you're responsible for teaching and speaking in front of others, and you are the spiritual leader of a group of people. Naturally, people look to you for answers. Your LGBTQ+ students are no exception. They have lots of questions and may have no other resources or support.

Yet, so often—dare we say most of time—you might not have all the answers. When adults find themselves in this position, they can take one of two roads:

ROAD #1: BLUFF.

Instead of risking the impression of not having the answers, some adults will react from a misinformed or underinformed place, falling back on opinions, experience, or hearsay rather than facts. Sometimes they get away with this with no harm done. But talking with an LGBTQ+ teenager is not the time to test that luck.

ROAD #2: DODGE.

When faced with a tough question, some adults squirm, redirect, or sweep the question under the rug. But once a queer teenager has confided in you, you become a powerful part of that young person's life. The last thing they need is for someone they trust to brush them off out of fear or ignorance.

A BETTER RESPONSE

We'd like to offer a third way, one rooted in self-awareness, humility, and openness. As important as it is to keep learning, it's also important to admit what you don't know. Take a moment to think about some questions or topics a young LGBTQ+ person might come to you with:

- ✦ "Do you know a counselor/therapist I should see?"
- ✦ "What do I tell my parents?"
- ✦ "Can I lie?"
- ✦ "How do I find a strong LGBTQ+ community in our town?"
- ✦ "What does [insert Bible passage] mean when it says . . . ?"

Do you know how to answer these? If not, do you know how to find answers? Do the other leaders in your church? Who would you point a young person to for their questions? It's important to think about these things now and prepare yourself before you've got a teenager in crisis sitting in your office.

Have a brainstorm session with your adult volunteers, or spend some time doing research online to come up with a list of questions that might come your way. Then, find the answers! As you recognize gaps in knowledge, don't shy away. Lean in to what you don't know. Educate yourself.

If you don't know where to start, consider the following topics:

- ✦ THE GENERATIONAL SHIFT: Life is different now than it was ten, twenty, or thirty years ago. The challenges and experiences facing youth are different. Learn about and think through what these differences are.

✦ **TEENAGE DEVELOPMENT:** Yep, we're talking psychology. You already know that adolescence is a unique time of social, emotional, intellectual, and physical change. For LGBTQ+ teenagers, these changes can be extra challenging. So brush up on your general understanding of adolescence, but focus on the ways LGBTQ+ teenagers experience puberty, dating, family relationships, etc.

✦ **THE LOCAL LGBTQ+ COMMUNITY:** Know the safe spaces, the advocates, the counselors, the educators, the equippers of LGBTQ+ teenagers in your area. These will be your go-to resources when you need help finding answers, or when your student is looking for other trusted adults to talk to.

✦ **SCHOOL POLICIES:** You likely have relationships with the administrators of the middle and high schools your students attend. This is a good time to find out more about how LGBTQ+ students are treated at these schools and what support is available for them. Know the names of the school mental health professionals and counselors. Find out about bathroom and locker room policies. Having this information will give you a good idea of what your students' daily experience is like and will help you point them to resources as needed.

✦ **THE LGBTQ+ COMMUNITY AT LARGE:** Be familiar with online resources, books, blogs, speakers, websites, forums, etc. that your LGBTQ+ students and families might be reading or participating in. Pay attention to news stories about LGBTQ+ people, celebrities who are out and proud, and other cultural conversations around LGBTQ+ inclusion and advocacy.

✦ **LGBTQ+ HEALTH AND SAFETY:** Teenagers and/or their families might come to you with questions about things like hormone blockers, STIs, gender-neutral bathrooms, sports involvement, and a host of other questions about the day-to-day experiences of being a queer teenager. You don't have to know all the ins and outs of these big issues, but you need to have at least a working knowledge of the concerns your students might face.

KNOW YOUR LIMITS

No matter how much you learn and how open you are to having conversations with your LGBTQ+ students, there will be times when you are just not the best resource for a young person. If you're straight and/or cisgender, it's just a fact. Sometimes queer teenagers *need* to talk to queer adults. Even if they don't yet realize it, there will be experiences you just can't step into.

But even when you're not the best resource, you might be the only resource a teenager has. This is why it's essential to offer help and support, even if it means saying, "I don't know, but we'll figure it out together."

Being honest about what you don't know is a way of affirming your LGBTQ+ youth. Not only does it model honesty and humility, but it demonstrates that there is something inherently queer about queerness. That not everyone *does understand*. It validates and supports your youth.

When you are up against your limits, be clear about why that's the case. This could be as simple as saying, "I don't have the experience in the transgender community necessary to answer that question. Let's find someone who does." In doing so, you're communicating that you care about the teenager's question even if you can't answer it yourself. Offer to walk alongside them, to join them in conversations with other people, to advocate for them wherever you can.

At the same time, check your personal and professional boundaries. You can't—and shouldn't—be your student's only source of support.

A FINAL THOUGHT

Keep checking in with your students, even when they've found reliable support outside of your ministry. They are going through a process and will appreciate knowing that you continue to walk through it with them. Remain open. Keep listening. Continue to be a safe person for your students.

At the same time, be sure to have regular conversations and interactions with your queer students that have nothing to do with their orientation or gender identity. LGBTQ+ people are too often reduced to their queerness. While that can be a big part of a person's identity, it's not all there is. Ask about your queer students' hobbies and interests, their friends, their summer vacation, their post–high school plans. See the whole person, not just the queer kid.

Bri, 23:

> If you are meeting with us because we are seeking information and validation, please be aware that many of us have already done a lot of independent research to try to justify our very existence to ourselves. I don't always want to hear the same things repeated back at me that the quickest web search can give me. I have already heard this and found it to be not enough. I need support and education on a deeper level. The more we can put these teachings out into the mainstream church so that I don't have to seek it out individually, the better.

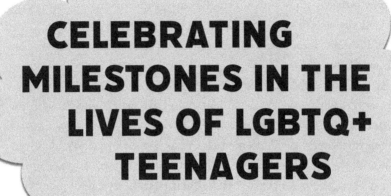

CELEBRATING MILESTONES IN THE LIVES OF LGBTQ+ TEENAGERS

You probably celebrate a lot of milestones with your students, some faith-based, some not—confirmation, starting high school, getting a driver's license, etc. Those celebrations are a great way to acknowledge the ways your students are growing and maturing and gaining new experiences. Being part of those moments is one of the joys of youth ministry.

For your LGBTQ+ students, however, there are some specific, life-changing milestones that not only go unnoticed but often are used to shame them. Whether you do it publicly or privately, we encourage you to start celebrating these milestones with joy and sincerity.

As with any teenager, a queer teen will have different events and moments they'd like to acknowledge. Here are just a few important milestones to be aware of:

★ Coming out, publicly, privately, or just to you

★ A name and/or pronoun change

★ First same-sex date or kiss or relationship

★ Transition milestones for trans and nonconforming youth

* Anything from piercing ears to starting puberty blockers
* Creating a Gay-Straight Alliance or LGBTQ+ support group

Ask your LGBTQ+ students if they want to have some kind of acknowledgment of these milestones and what that might look like. Even if they don't want to do anything, showing them that you understand the importance of these events is a huge sign of your support.

Celebrating can be as simple as a heartfelt "Good for you!" or "Congratulations! I'm really proud of you." Or it can be a full-on party. Whatever the milestone, however big or small, ask the individual how they would like to celebrate. Who would they like to include? Should this be a small group of close friends? A family gathering? A churchwide celebration? A card? Scale your celebrations appropriately, based on what the young person is comfortable with.

WORSHIP SERVICE CELEBRATIONS

Along with some of the big-picture milestones in an LGBTQ+ student's life, your church might consider some kind of communal ceremony for a queer person who has claimed a new identity or undergone a physical transformation. There are plenty of ways to honor this change. Work with your church staff to consider what it could look like for a young person to publicly affirm or claim their baptism in light of their new identity. Offer to develop prayers or liturgical expressions around such a celebration. Some denominations already have name change liturgies. Invite the student to make a statement during your confirmation service or on Youth Sunday. Whatever you decide, be sure to include plenty of input from your student and their family.

Such a celebration once doesn't mean a queer teenager's journey is over. Rather, it's an opportunity to usher them into what's next and instill in them a sense of self-worth and confidence. Over time, even simple actions will create a space in your youth group and church where affirmation and celebration of all the big moments in your students' lives are the norm.

Kai, 21:

While my first instinct [about what LGBTQ+ milestones churches should celebrate] was to say "coming out," I hope in a few years that coming out will be deemed unnecessary, and people are expected to love who they love, regardless of gender. Church leaders in particular should celebrate marriages in the LGBTQ+ community and work towards having these ceremonies in their own church. Queer youth should know that they are loved and accepted just as they are from the moment they step through the church doors.

Gaby, 23:

The obvious answer [to what milestones churches should celebrate] is coming out, but I think there are also smaller, quieter, personal milestones and moments that are worth appreciating and celebrating both before and after someone comes out for the first time. For example, the first time you can think "I am queer, and that's okay" without a disclaimer or a feeling of dishonesty. When you find your group of people who love and support you, whether that be your blood family or your chosen one. The first time you don't hesitate before coming out to someone new in the middle of a sentence, because slipping in, "I'm going to see my girlfriend later," isn't a big deal anymore. When a loved one acknowledges and validates your identity easily and you feel warm long after the moment has passed. When your queerness is no longer your whole identity and just another beautiful part of who you are.

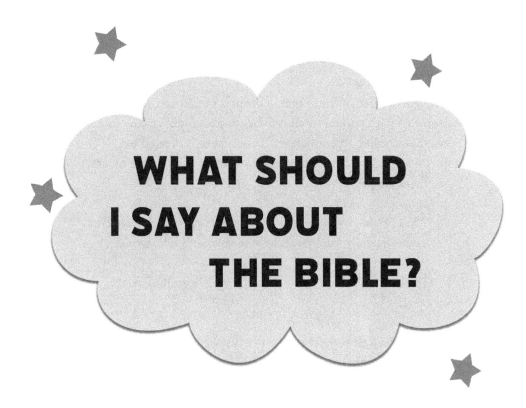

WHAT SHOULD I SAY ABOUT THE BIBLE?

You already know that a subset of Christians have been using the seven so-called "clobber passages" in Scripture to invalidate the identity of queer people for a very, very long time. They argue that the concepts of trans and nonconforming identities are modern inventions, that same-sex relationships are explicitly forbidden, and that both are contrary to the will of a God who created male and female and designed marriage to be between one man and one woman.

As we said earlier, there are lots of great resources that explain why that perspective is not an accurate reading of the Bible, so we're not going to unpack all of that here. Instead, we want to offer examples of the places where the Bible affirms the value of queer people.

Even if your church is affirming and inclusive, your students are inevitably going to face people who want to use the Bible as a weapon to shame and condemn them. Sharing these stories and passages with your students is more than just a way to encourage them. It's a way to help them hold both their faith and their identity as two essential parts of themselves even when others tell them they can't.

BIBLE VERSES

GENESIS 1:26: In the very first chapter of Genesis, God is described with plural pronouns. "Let us make humankind in our image, according to our likeness." Each of us is created in this full image of God, making us more complex than simple binary gender delineations would suggest.

PSALM 139: God knows who we are even before we are born. God formed us, fearfully and wonderfully, to be exactly who we are.

ISAIAH 43:1: We are God's, from the very beginning to the very end.

ISAIAH 56:3–5: Eunuchs were not allowed in the temple because they were sexual minorities. But God includes them in God's family, giving them "an everlasting name that shall not be cut off."

MATTHEW 22:37–40: Love God; love our neighbors. This is what it looks like to follow Jesus. That's the will of God. When people treat others with anything less than love, they aren't honoring these commandments.

ACTS 8:26–40: The eunuch from Ethiopia, who was a foreigner, a sexual minority, and not Jewish, was baptized by Philip simply because he asked to be. This story tells us that the community of Christ includes people society considers to be outcasts.

ACTS 10:1–11:18: In this long and kind of weird story, God shows Peter that relationships are more important than the purity laws of Moses. Peter has to overcome a belief he has held his whole life in order to follow God's command to love others. This is a big deal.

GALATIANS 3:28: Paul tells us that the religious and cultural barriers that once separated people from each other fall away when we are followers of Jesus. "There is no longer male and female; for all of you are one in Christ Jesus." That'll preach.

BIBLE CHARACTERS

NAOMI AND RUTH: Naomi was Ruth's mother-in-law until Ruth's husband died. But rather than head back to her home country, which would have been the normal next step, Ruth decided to stay with Naomi. While that in itself doesn't suggest anything other than friendship, it is interesting that the Bible uses the same Hebrew word (dabaq, which basically means "to cleave") for Ruth's feelings for Naomi as it does for Adam's feelings for Eve. If nothing else, this story honors the closeness of two women who love each other.

DAVID AND JONATHAN: The relationship between David and Jonathan has been held up as an example of same-sex love for centuries. While no one knows if theirs was a sexual relationship, they clearly shared a deep, intimate love for one another, a love blessed by God. In 2 Samuel 1:26, David mourns Jonathan, saying, "Greatly beloved were you to me; your love to me was wonderful, passing the love of women." The Bible doesn't shy away from the importance of their love and care for one another, and it never hints that there was anything unusual or shameful about their relationship, which suggests their same-sex love might not have been unique.

THE BELOVED DISCIPLE: There is a long line of scholarship that suggests that John (or someone) had a special relationship with Jesus. While we aren't going to speculate on the ins and outs of that relationship, it is interesting to know that the idea that this "beloved disciple" was more than a friend shows up as early as the twelfth century. Again, we're not taking a side on this, but simply pointing out that reading queer relationships into the Bible is not new. At all.

PAUL: Was Paul gay? Who knows? But we do know that Paul never married, which was unusual for a Jewish man, and that he refers to "a thorn . . . given me in the flesh" (2 Corinthians 12:7), indicating some kind of inner battle. There's not enough evidence to say Paul was or wasn't gay, but we often see him wrestling with his own past and trying to work out what it means to live faithfully as a flawed human being. Teenagers—queer and straight alike—can look to Paul for an example of someone who is working out how to live as a follower of Jesus even as they make mistakes.

NAME CHANGES IN SCRIPTURE

Trans kids will likely consider a name change before undergoing any medical procedures. It may help them to know that name changes occur many times in Scripture. Abram/Abraham and Sarai/Sarah (Genesis 17), Jacob/Israel (Genesis 32), Simon/Peter (Matthew 16), and Hosea/Joshua (Numbers 13) are all examples of important people from the Bible to whom God gave a new name to reflect a new identity.

GOD AND GENDER

While the Bible is very clear that God doesn't have a gender, the limits of language and patriarchal religious systems have led to centuries of male imagery for God in our prayers and creeds, in art and music. And while there are plenty of places where the Bible refers to God as "Father," there are also lots of places where the writers use feminine images for God. Lady Wisdom, described in Proverbs 8, is understood to be God's cocreator from the very beginning who is still at work today. The word *Elohim* is considered a plural noun and is commonly found in the Old Testament as a name for God. The Holy Trinity expresses God in three persons—another nod toward God being "they." God is described as giving birth and nursing a child in Deuteronomy 32 and as comforting people like a mother in Isaiah 66. Even Jesus wants to gather Jerusalem "as a hen gathers her brood" (Matthew 23:37).

This isn't revolutionary stuff, and you've probably talked about some of this with your students in the past. But connecting this ungendered language for God to the experiences of LGBTQ+ teenagers can be hugely affirming and can help them start to see their gender identity as reflecting a unique image of God.

QUEER PEOPLE IN THE EARLY CHURCH

We don't know much about the orientations of most historical figures, especially in the church. Still, there are some people in the history of the church who wrote or spoke about queer identities and relationships in ways that tell us something about the commonality of queerness in Christian history.

As you read through these examples, keep in mind that orientation is about attraction, not just sex. In other words, a lesbian is a woman who is attracted to other women, whether or not she ever has sex with one. So when we tell you about nuns who loved other women, or monks who loved other men, we're not saying they broke their vows or were sneaking around. And we're not speculating on their orientation. We're highlighting these stories as a tool for helping queer teenagers find themselves in the history of their faith.

> **ST. AELRED:** The patron saint of friendship was an abbot in twelfth-century England. While he promoted chastity, he also wrote glowingly about the beauty of intimate male friendships. He wrote, "A man who can shed tears with you in your worries, be happy with you when things go well, search out with you the answers to your problems, whom with the ties of charity you can lead into the depths of your heart; . . . where the sweetness of the Spirit flows between you, where you so join yourself and cleave to him that soul mingles with soul and two become one."

> **AUGUSTINE OF HIPPO:** Augustine is known for his views on sex and original sin, but there are scholars who believe some

of his strident warnings about sex grew out of his own repressed sexuality. In his Confessions, Augustine writes movingly about the death of a male friend from his youth, saying, "I felt that my soul and my friend's had been one soul in two bodies."

Augustine also wrote about intersex people in his book City of God. In a discussion of what he calls "androgyni," Augustine writes, "God, the Creator of all, knows where and when each thing ought to be, or to have been created, because He sees the similarities and diversities which can contribute to the beauty of the whole."

SOR JUANA INÉS DE LA CRUZ: A Mexican nun who lived in the late 1600s, Sister Juana entered the convent because women weren't allowed to go to university. It is believed she had, if not a full-on affair, at least a very close friendship with a Mexican countess. Sor Juana wrote romantic poetry for the countess, with stanzas like this:

> Let my love be ever doomed
> if guilty in its intent,
> for loving you is a crime
> of which I will never repent.

ST. BERNARD OF CLAIRVAUX: Bernard, an eleventh-century French monk, wrote songs, poems, and sermons, many of which can only be described as erotic poetry about Jesus. Using imagery not unlike what we find in the Song of Songs, Bernard spoke eloquently of his intense love for Jesus. He also wrote of his intense love for an Irish primate (basically a bishop) named Malachy. Bernard wrote of kissing Malachy and of the two of them traveling to see one another. When Malachy died, Bernard wore the habit in which his friend died to his funeral and was buried in it when he died five years later.

HILDEGARD OF BINGEN: A nun from the eleventh century, Hildegard had a very close relationship with Richardis von Stade, a young woman who became Hildegard's personal assistant. Whether or not they had a sexual relationship, Hildegard's writings make it clear that Richardis was the woman she loved.

JOAN OF ARC: Joan was a teenager, and while we don't know anything about her sexual orientation, we do know that she was unafraid to push gender norms to the side for what she believed in. And she believed God was calling her to dress in men's clothes, which was illegal. She was queer before queer was cool.

A FINAL THOUGHT

We don't offer these examples so you can start an argument or cherry-pick your favorite Bible verses. Scripture isn't a weapon—for conservatives or progressives. Instead, we hope this information helps you show the queer students in your group that the witness of Bible characters and early church leaders is for them too.

WHAT IS A SAFE SPACE? HOW DO I CREATE ONE?

So much of youth ministry is tied to the physical, emotional, and spiritual space created for teenagers. But creating a safe and welcoming space for LGBTQ+ students is not the same as designing a super-trendy, snack-friendly, tech-savvy youth room. Unfortunately, you can't choose group dynamics like you can choose a paint color scheme. You can't throw out people's biases like those old couch cushions. But don't be discouraged! There are many practical steps you can take to create a space that's safe and welcoming for your LGBTQ+ students and their families.

SAFE SPACE? REALLY?

A quick word about the idea of safe spaces: they have gotten some bad press in the last few years as some groups push back against the idea that people need protection from offensive ideas or words. Maybe you've even thought to yourself, "We can't guard kids' feelings all the time or they'll never learn to stand up for themselves." But creating safe spaces is less about guarding a person's feelings and more about creating a different culture of behavior.

Believe us when we say that queer teenagers face a culture that wants to shame, demean, or erase them at just about every turn. There are very few truly safe spaces to be a queer teenager, and your LGBTQ+ students are demonstrating their resilience constantly. So don't fall for that narrative that says you're coddling kids or not preparing them for the real world. No one is more aware of the challenges the world presents than LGBTQ+ teenagers.

You, on the other hand, can create a place where they can let their guard down. Where they can relax and know they are fully seen, loved, and respected just as they are. You can demonstrate the endless, boundless love of God by showing them that they are worth the work it takes to make a safe space for them. That is a tremendous gift to give a young person, regardless of their sexuality or gender identity. It is a rare and precious experience for a queer teenager.

THE DATA

Home:

 49% of LGBTQ+ teens say they have an adult family member they could turn to for help.

 25% say they can "definitely be themselves" at home.

School:

 27% of LGBTQ+ students report that they can "definitely be themselves" at school.

 5% say teachers and school staff are supportive of LGBTQ+ people.

Church:

 8% of church-going LGBTQ+ youth are out at church.

 35% say they "know" their place of worship is not accepting of LGBTQ+ people.

Human Rights Campaign

These numbers represent the LGBTQ+ community as a whole. Depending on individual and context, they can look very different.

TAKING INVENTORY

The first step in providing such a meaningful experience is taking inventory of your current space:

THE PHYSICAL SPACE

★ Is there room for people to sit alone without being isolated, or is all the seating on couches or arranged in groups?

★ What kinds of images are on the walls? If they include people, do they represent a broad range of genders and ethnicities? If they have affirming messages, are those messages true for everyone? Do they reflect the real experience of being in this group?

★ What's your bathroom and/or locker room situation? Is there a safe and private option for trans and nonconforming individuals?

★ What books, videos, music, or other resources are available for students to use? Do they only apply to straight or cisgender students? Think about books on dating or videos about drug use that you've been using for years. Can everyone in your group see and hear from people like them in these materials?

★ Do the songs you sing or the prayers you use employ gendered language for God?

THE EMOTIONAL SPACE

★ What language do you and your volunteers use around gender? Do you recognize names and pronouns? Do you use words or terms that assume binary gender or straight orientation (for example, "you guys," "ladies and gentlemen")?

- Is this an assumption-free space, meaning you don't assume everyone is straight?

- How are groups and teams organized during activities? How would a queer student know which group they belong to?

- Does your ministry include gender-specific activities, like a boys' Bible study or a girls' small group? Where would a nonbinary student fit into these?

- Do any of your activities rely on gender stereotypes around dress or behavior?

- What is your group's atmosphere around physical touch? Are you a hug-heavy, back-rubbing, hand-holding group? How would a student let you know they are uncomfortable with this kind of touch? How would a student be treated by others if they didn't take part in these activities?

- What kind of dress code do you have? Is it gender-neutral? What's the rationale behind any rules you have? Is that rationale based on assumptions about behavior or on actual behavior?

- Do the adult volunteers align with your core values? Will they affirm and accept everyone in your youth group, and follow any codes or standards you have for inclusive language and behavior?

- What rules do you have around confidentiality in both group and private conversations?

THE SPIRITUAL SPACE

- What language do you use for God? Do leaders address God in prayer through multiple names (Father, Mother, Creator, Provider, Friend, etc.)?

- How do you talk about bodies, sex, and relationships? What is being communicated about God and issues like purity, marriage, and virginity?

* How do you communicate God's love and care for all of your students?
* Does the rest of your church hold the same values around sexuality as what are being communicated in your group, or will students experience a disconnect between what they hear from you and what they hear from the pulpit?
* How do you equip families to communicate God's love and care for their teenagers?

THE VALUE OF A SAFE SPACE

Safe spaces aren't just for queer teenagers—they benefit everyone. All of your students will grow by learning how to welcome, affirm, and accept people of all sexual orientations and gender identities. Your non-LGBTQ+ students will be more comfortable inviting their queer friends (because, yes, they have queer friends) to church when they know their friends will be valued and loved. And your straight and cis students will be grateful for a space that doesn't reduce them to gender stereotypes or limit them to narrow ideas about their bodies and relationships.

Teenagers are actively developing their mindsets and worldviews. They are looking at you for how to love, accept, and communicate with people who are different than them. By creating a safe space now, you're setting up your students to be mature, open-hearted adults. (And we definitely need more of those.)

THREATS TO A SAFE SPACE

Threats to a safe space don't have to be intentional or aggressive to do harm. As you deepen your relationships with your LGBTQ+ students, you'll be more tuned in to microaggressions and sources of exclusion when they happen. And you'll be more prepared to advocate for your queer youth when they need you to.

The most obvious threats are overt bullying (physical and verbal), exclusion by other students or volunteers, and language that conveys shame and guilt about identity. What you perceive as little slights, like not respecting names and pronouns, or making passive, negative comments about queer people, might seem irrelevant to a lot of people.

Such occurrences may seem "not worth the effort" to call out every time they happen. But they are loud, neon signs flashing the message "You don't belong here!" to your LGBTQ+ students.

Don't let these comments or exclusions slide by. Call them out firmly and gracefully. Use these moments as opportunities to inspire your students and volunteers to a higher standard of kindness and respect.

As with many of the suggestions in this book, this is another place where planning ahead will have a big payoff. Think now about how you want to handle the inevitable cruel joke or rude comment aimed at one of your queer students. Have a plan, make sure your volunteers know what it is, and communicate it clearly to the whole group. Follow through on whatever consequences you decide are appropriate, and work with the people involved to move toward healing and restored relationships.

RECOMMENDATIONS

If you want to create a safe space, consider these steps:

- ✦ Educate staff, volunteers, and yourself on language and microaggressions around sexuality, gender, race, disability, etc. Do this annually, as these conventions may change over time. Set a policy for the language, values, and conduct you expect of staff and volunteers. Have clear consequences for violations.

- ✦ Review traditions, small group activities, icebreakers, and games for unnecessary binaries.

- ✦ Review your sexuality curriculum. Use one that's inclusive and doesn't make assumptions about gender or sexuality, such as Our Whole Lives.

- ✦ Require consent for activities that involve touching—or eliminate such activities entirely.

- ✦ Create a group covenant that all leaders and students sign that articulates your group's core values, treatment of each other, use of language, and response to insensitive behavior.

A FINAL THOUGHT

Safe spaces don't magically appear even if you have all the best intentions and do good and careful work. More often, safe spaces are the natural result of time spent getting to know, respect, and celebrate the LGBTQ+ students in your group. As these relationships deepen, it's likely you'll naturally start to create safe spaces that demonstrate love, acceptance, and a desire to protect these vulnerable students.

Kate, 23:

There isn't ever really a 100% safe space, because people can always say hurtful things, even unintentionally, but the safest places I've found are where I feel free to be the most myself and know it'll be answered with love and support. I don't want to befriend people who try & gain my trust in the short term with the hope that in the long term they can bestow their "truth" and change my mind. I don't want spaces where I feel like I can't discuss my romantic life or sexuality.

Someone once said to me, "Christian spaces find harmony when everyone believes the same thing. That's how people grow together." In some sense I understand that—but we need to be allowed to choose. If we're rejected for our differences, for choosing a different way, for questioning the way things have been, that isn't a safe space.

Heather, 21:

If anybody is looking to start a Queer Christian group, I would advise making sure that you reach out to youth, that you use social media as a tool, that you don't allow hatred from either community, and that you are nonjudgmental and inclusive. Not everyone in our group is Queer; some are allies. Not everyone in our group is Christian; some really struggle with their faith. We welcome them all anyways, and so should everyone. The love that God has for every one of His children overrides any and all identity that we may see as abnormal, and it's important to convey that to the people who need to hear it the most.

Graham, 28:

> Create a space where people are accepted and celebrated without conditions, not just tolerated. Ask LGBTQ+ youth what they like about themselves, why they feel God gave them this unique trait, and what they've learned from it. It's so important for these youth to realize that being LGBTQ+ is part of whatever path God made for them, rather than a mistake or defect that they are somehow at fault for.
>
> Scripture is full of people who had to grapple with being different or ostracized and is usually accompanied by a reassurance that God hasn't left their side for a minute. I find these types of narratives very encouraging in an LGBTQ+ context, and they might be a much-needed source of strength and a good topic of discussion. Include non-LGBTQ+ youth in some of these conversations, too, so that you create a more understanding and loving church community in general.

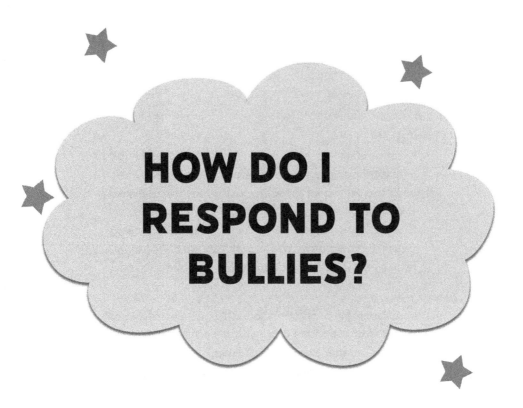

HOW DO I RESPOND TO BULLIES?

Unfortunately, no matter how much work you put into creating your safe space, you're going to encounter bullies and victims of bullying in your group.

Bullying gets a lot of attention, but it's worth taking a minute to ask a basic question: What is bullying? The organization Stomp Out Bullying says bullying occurs "when someone hurts or scares another person repeatedly." It can include:

- ★ Hurtful or derogatory names
- ★ Spreading lies and rumors about someone
- ★ Being cruel or teasing someone
- ★ Hitting, punching, shoving, spitting, or other physical attacks
- ★ "Ganging up" on others
- ★ Stealing money or other items
- ★ Threatening harm

Bullying affects all teenagers, and bullies can be of any age or profession. Even some parents, pastors, and teachers, in addition to peers, bully teenagers. LGBTQ+ teenagers in particular are targeted throughout their middle school and high school years.

THE NUMBERS ON BULLYING

73% of LGBTQ+ youth have experienced verbal threats because of their actual or perceived LGBTQ+ identity.

Human Rights Campaign

3 in 10 LGBTQ+ youth have received physical threats due to their LGBTQ+ identity.

Human Rights Campaign

70% of LGBTQ+ youth have been bullied at their school because of their sexual orientation;

Human Rights Campaign

Each step toward the most gender nonconforming end of the spectrum is associated with 15% greater odds of being bullied in school and electronically.

Williams Institute

The prevalence of having not gone to school because of safety concerns was higher among LGBTQ+ students (10%) than among those who identified as heterosexual (6%).

Centers for Disease Control and Prevention

The prevalence of being bullied online was also higher among students identifying as lesbian and bisexual female (29%) than among those identifying as gay and bisexual male (22%).

Centers for Disease Control and Prevention

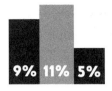

9% 11% 5%

The prevalence of having been threatened or injured with a weapon on school property was higher among students who identified as gay, lesbian, and bisexual (9%) or not sure (11%) than among those who identified as heterosexual (5%).

Centers for Disease Control and Prevention

WHAT'S CURRENTLY BEING DONE TO ADDRESS BULLYING

Legislation is one of the most powerful tools for protecting queer youth from bullies, and it is crucial that faith communities engage in advocacy for legislation protecting teenagers from discrimination and harassment based on sexual orientation and gender.

States with anti-bullying laws that specifically protect LGBTQ+ teenagers have fewer suicide attempts among *all* teenagers, not just LGBTQ+ teenagers.[25]

However, to date, only twenty-one states and the District of Columbia have enacted laws specifically to protect LGBTQ+ teenagers from being bullied by students, teachers, or school staff because of their sexual orientation and gender identity.[26] Many local municipalities and schools are also creating anti-bullying policies, despite inaction at the state level. Reach out to your local, state, and federal representatives and ask them to take action on passing anti-bullying laws.

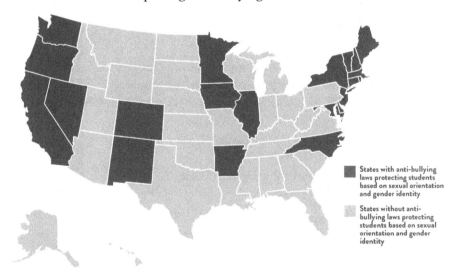

States with anti-bullying laws protecting students based on sexual orientation and gender identity

States without anti-bullying laws protecting students based on sexual orientation and gender identity

BUILDING A COMMUNITY-BASED POLICY

While larger-scale action is certainly important, it's imperative that you also address bullying within your youth group and congregation. As always, it's best to be proactive and anticipate where and how bullying might occur. If you've done the work of creating a safe space for LGBTQ+ students, hopefully you've already identified situations that might lead to bullying and exclusion. But you know your group better than anyone and are uniquely aware of group dynamics that could create problems.

If bullying is taking place within your group, you're in the tricky spot of being the youth leader for both the bully and the bullied. That means you have an obligation to tend to the deeper issues behind any bullying incident. That might mean helping to find counseling for a student who is persistently aggressive, working with families who disagree with your definition of bullying, and potentially uncovering abuse or other forms of mistreatment in the lives of your students. This is all the more reason to work with your church staff, maybe a counselor or mental health professional from the high school, or families as you develop an anti-bullying policy that's clear, consistent, and enforceable.

If you don't already have a policy around bullying for your group, it's time to put one together. Your policy should include incidents that happen while you're at church, as well as bullying that occurs on trips, during service projects, at camp, or during other off-site activities. Here are some suggestions to get you started:

+ **CLEARLY DELINEATE WHAT IS AND IS NOT CONSIDERED BULLYING.** Be specific enough to be able to spot it instantly, but broad enough to include any possibility of bullying you weren't able to predict or anticipate. Make sure students and staff understand these definitions.

+ **USE YOUR GROUP COVENANT OR CHURCH POLICY AS A STARTING POINT FOR YOUR POLICY.** This can also be a helpful tool when you approach the person doing the bullying to remind them that their actions don't line up with the agreement they made for how students in your group will treat each other. Having that basis will go a long way toward helping you address these issues.

✤ **BE CLEAR ABOUT WHO WILL APPROACH AN AGGRESSOR AND IN WHAT SETTING.** One-on-one conversations are far more effective than public scolding that can embarrass a student or escalate the situation.

✤ **BE PREPARED TO INVOLVE FAMILIES OR LEGAL AUTHORITIES WHEN APPROPRIATE.**

✤ **DANGEROUS AND PERSISTENT BULLYING IS ILLEGAL AND NEEDS TO BE TREATED AS SUCH.**

✤ **IDENTIFY A MEDIATOR WHO CAN HELP BRING RECONCILIATION BETWEEN AGGRESSOR AND VICTIM.** But remember that not every victim of bullying will want to meet with their aggressor. Don't force these conversations.

✤ **GET INPUT FROM YOUR LGBTQ+ STUDENTS.** They might have great ideas for how they'd like you to handle situations. For example, they might not want you to draw attention to a bullying incident in front of the group. And they might have done work in another group they're involved in, like a Gay-Straight Alliance, that can inform the policy you're creating.

RESPONDING IN THE MOMENT

Policies are all well and good, but you also need to be prepared to respond in the moment when you observe acts of bullying. This can be difficult, especially when you're leading an activity or teaching in a large group and are trying to keep a group focused. If you've gotten the okay from your LGBTQ+ students, call out the aggressive behavior in a firm but nonthreatening way.

For example, if a student uses a slur to make fun of an LGBTQ+ student, don't call them a name or escalate the situation by yelling. Instead, create a teachable moment where aggressor, victim, and bystanders can all learn why this action was wrong. You've set clear expectations for acceptable behavior in your group; now is the time to hold them to it.

When the bullying behavior comes from a student, always convey empathy when confronting them. They are still teenagers who are learning, growing, and possibly lashing out in their own pain. Oftentimes the people who are acting like bullies are the victims of bullying at home, school, or other settings. They are still a part of your group and they are loved by God. Meet with them privately to give them space to express their feelings and work with you to understand why they've acted a certain way. And while it sounds cliché, it's true that some homophobic people are actually wrestling with their own sexuality. Don't assume that's the case, but it is something to be aware of and sensitive to.

Always be sure to check in with the student being bullied. You might see one instance of bullying one time during the week, but your student might be getting a steady stream of it outside of your group. So talk to them, assure them of their value, and find out how they're dealing with these attacks. Involve a counselor or their family when you sense the bullying is taking a toll on them. And do not blame them for what happens. They get to talk and dress and look and act in ways that are authentic to their identity.

Here's the hard part: sometimes you'll need to allow (and monitor) conversations between the two parties so they can air out their reactions and responses. Be sensitive to the needs of all people, and give space for honest interaction, questions, and opportunities for growth. Resist the urge to immediately interrupt or interject when the conversation gets tough. You're there to prevent further aggression but not to prevent difficult conversations. The tough times may bring deeper healing and growth to the individuals involved.

Remember:

- ✦ No one deserves to be bullied.
- ✦ Being themselves is never an excuse for someone to be mistreated.
- ✦ It's not their responsibility to "stick it out."

- ★ Despite your most fervent and loving attempt to make someone feel safe, they may not come back. That is their choice; respect it.

WHAT ABOUT CYBERBULLYING?

Cyberbullying is a whole other issue. As you know, it's an increasingly popular way for young aggressors to lash out at their peers.

Cyberbullying doesn't always look like angry hate speech. It can show up in more subtle ways, like spreading false rumors about someone, posting pictures without consent for the purpose of embarrassment or humiliation, or sharing private information without consent. While this is a huge issue for all teenagers, here again LGBTQ+ teens are at particular risk of experiencing cyberbullying.

Take a look at these statistics:

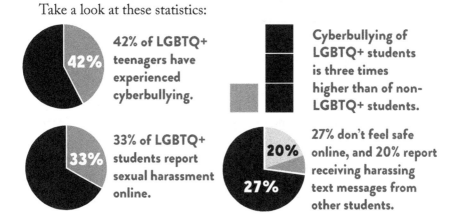

42% of LGBTQ+ teenagers have experienced cyberbullying.

Cyberbullying of LGBTQ+ students is three times higher than of non-LGBTQ+ students.

33% of LGBTQ+ students report sexual harassment online.

27% don't feel safe online, and 20% report receiving harassing text messages from other students.

Netsanity: Cyberbullying: LGBTQ Youth

Cyberbullying presents unique challenges that are often difficult to address. It is often persistent and ubiquitous; it can happen all day, every day, across multiple venues. It can seem impossible for the victim to find relief. In addition, information and photos shared through cyberbullying are permanent and public. This can drastically affect a young person's reputation in the immediate and distant future. Finally, cyberbullying is hard to notice, especially for adults who don't live in the digital space occupied by teenagers.

The damaging behavior can't be overheard or witnessed or recorded, which makes responding to cyberbullying a particularly daunting task.[27]

Despite these challenges, you are still responsible for responding to cyberbullying once you are made aware of it occurring among your youth group. If you suspect or are informed of someone being cyberbullied, take these steps:

✦ **SPEAK TO THE VICTIM PRIVATELY ABOUT IT.** Ask if they have proof on their phone or digital devices that they are willing to share (advise them to screenshot everything).

✦ **SPEAK TO A PARENT.** You may need to serve as a facilitator between children, parents, and the school, if necessary.

✦ **IF APPROPRIATE, ADDRESS THE AGGRESSOR AND THEIR PARENTS.** Let them know this behavior is not tolerated in your group. Adhere to your anti-bullying policy as you explain consequences and disciplinary action.

✦ **KNOW THE LAW.** Some forms of cyberbullying veer into harassment, abuse, or even child pornography territory. And parents, who technically own the phones their kids use, can be held liable for images and messages sent from "their" devices. Be sure parents understand the very real consequences of turning a blind eye to cyberbullying.

Too many victims of cyberbullying attempt suicide because they see no other end to the abuse. Be firm and take immediate action. If you think a young person may be having suicidal thoughts, direct them to immediate sources of help:

★ **National Suicide Prevention Hotline: 1-800-273-8255**
★ **Trans Lifeline: 877-565-8860**
★ **Trevor Project Lifeline: 1-866-488-7386**

In order to address the growing and unique concerns of cyberbullying, take time to learn about the digital platforms on which your young people are hanging out. Have open and honest discussions about cyberbullying with your students. Talk about how cyberbullying goes against your group's covenant, and encourage students to stand up against cyberbullying when they see it occurring. Invite students to share their stories of cyberbullying. Ask them how they can avoid participating in, condoning, or overlooking cyberbullying when they see it.

A FINAL THOUGHT ON BULLYING

It's impossible for you to be aware of every single instance of bullying that happens among the people in your group. More often than not, you'll find out about previous incidents rather than witness them firsthand. So before bullying ever occurs, your students need to see your staff being advocates for their LGBTQ+ peers and taking a zero-tolerance stance on bullying and harassment. Model the culture you want to create in the group—one where bullying is not tolerated, and where everyone feels safe and welcome.

> *K., 18:*
>
> When an LGBTQ+ person is being bullied, do and say something. Tell the person being bullied that it's going to be ok, and just as importantly, tell the bully that what they're doing isn't ok, and have them face actual consequences for their actions.

CAN I STILL HAVE GENDERED ACTIVITIES?

Splitting students by gender is an easy way of dividing groups of people, especially in youth group activities. Boys-vs.-girls skit night, girls' small groups and boys' small groups, or guys' game night and girls' spa night. The cultural norms and expectations of gender make it a natural divider for activities, education, social circles, and hobbies. And if you're someone who fits into those straight, cisgender norms, you've maybe never thought about the ways such divisions can create stress and exclusion for trans, gender nonconforming, and nonbinary people.

Even when the activity itself isn't centered on gender, gendered groups and activities force people to choose a binary they might not identify with, or to make a public selection, which they might not feel comfortable doing. Creating activities that require queer students to spend time in a group they don't feel they belong in is immediately excluding for the student. Even an innocuous activity suddenly becomes a reminder to a queer student that they don't fit in, that something about them isn't "normal."

And here's the thing: Gendered activities don't just affect LGBTQ+ teenagers. Gendered activities tend to limit engagement for students who, regardless of orientation, don't conform to gender stereotypes. Not every male, straight or otherwise, wants to play a rowdy game of football. Not every female is going to want to paint her nails and talk about romance movies. Phrases like "Boys will be boys" and "You throw like a girl" reinforce unhealthy and unrealistic gender norms for every student in your group.

That said, there will probably be activities and conversations where it does make sense to organize around gender. For example, maybe you want to bring in a speaker who talks with the girls in your group about their experiences of sexual harassment at school. Or maybe you want to include adult mentors in your ministry, and church policy requires these to be same-sex mentorships.

But even in these situations, it's possible to take gender out of the equation. Have a mentoring model that's not dependent on one-on-one meetings and therefore takes gender off the table. Make conversations around sex, dating, and consent open to everyone, and let students self-select their involvement. Whenever you think an activity or conversation needs to be gendered, ask yourself: "Why do I think this? Does this *really* need to be gendered, or is this just what we've always done?"

Everyone will benefit from your church breaking down gender barriers and inviting all voices into conversations.

A FINAL THOUGHT

As you consider new ways of grouping, debrief these changes with your students. What are the benefits of nongendered groups and activities? What challenges might the group face? How can they address those challenges? Check in with your LGBTQ+ students, especially trans and nonbinary kids, before and after activities. Ask questions like "Did you feel comfortable during that activity?" and "What would have made that experience better for you?" Make sure you're fostering healthy communication as you introduce changes and integrate across genders.

HOW DO I FIND AN INCLUSIVE SEX ED CURRICULUM?

For all our talk about the sacredness of sex and about our bodies as God's temple, the church hasn't always done a great job of speaking openly about either of them. This is especially true when it comes to teenagers, and even more so for queer teenagers. No matter what your church believes about hetero, queer, premarital, or extramarital sex, it's essential to be having conversations with youth about sexuality.

And by conversations, we mean more than a yearly sex talk or occasional guest speaker. Many of your students are actively exploring this part of their identity. And LGBTQ+ kids are unlikely to be getting safe, healthy information about sexuality anywhere. This has led to a startling gap in unsafe-sex practices between LGBTQ+ and heterosexual teens. Take a look at these numbers:

Only 12% of LGBTQ+ students received information about safe sex that was relevant to them as an LGBTQ+ person.[28]

Human Rights Campaign

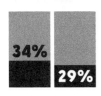 LGB students were more likely to be currently sexually active (33.7%) than their heterosexual peers (28.5%).[29]

Centers for Disease Control and Prevention

 LGB students were at least two times more likely to have sexual intercourse before age 13 and to not have used any method of pregnancy prevention.
CDC

 LGBTQ+ students were significantly less likely to have used condoms, birth control pills, or other contraceptive methods before or during their last sexual experience.
CDC

  Gay, lesbian, and bisexual teenagers were more likely to have had four or more sexual partners than heterosexual and questioning students.
CDC

These numbers, paired with a lack of education or information about safe sex and healthy relationships for LGBTQ+ youth, lead to dangerous scenarios. Queer students are two to three times more likely to experience physical and sexual dating violence than heterosexual students. LGBTQ+ students are more likely to participate in risky sexual experiences than heterosexual students. And queer students reported higher instances of date rape, violence, or abuse in dating relationships than their heterosexual peers.[30]

Having relevant, gender-inclusive sex ed curriculum isn't just a trendy idea. It's a safety issue. Some of your students, queer and nonqueer, are going to have sex. If you're not equipping them with the knowledge of appropriate safe-sex practices, they're likely to find information from other sources that don't have their best interests at heart. Don't leave their education to the internet or to a predator who might use their naiveté or lack of awareness to their advantage.

RECOMMENDATIONS

If you aren't currently using a sex ed curriculum, look for one that includes the following:

★ A shame-free approach. If the only sex ed message is "Don't do it until you're married," you're not actually equipping your students to make healthy decisions now.

★ Gender-inclusive language.

★ Regular mentions of t same-sex relationships and sexual activity, as well as ransgender and gender nonconforming education.

★ A holistic understanding of sex, sexuality, and relationships. Look for curriculum that addresses a range of topics from body image to dating relationships to gender orientation.

★ The use of Scripture, spiritual history, and teaching that aligns with your congregation's values and theology.

★ The inclusion of adults (namely, parents) as a support system for teenagers who have questions about the topic of sex.

If you're already using a curriculum:

★ Audit it for the above characteristics.

★ Actively change gender-exclusive language.

★ Fill in the gaps of this resource with activities and information from other sources.

★ Tweak stories, examples, and graphics to include all genders and orientations.

★ Make sure the overall message is about grace and love.

A FINAL THOUGHT

Make sure your group knows that talking about sex and sexuality isn't a one-time deal. This isn't just some awkward annual tradition they have to suffer through. Ask your students what they want to know and what they aren't hearing enough about. Encourage these authentic conversations as a part of your group's ethos. This doesn't mean you should be cracking sex jokes or winking innuendoes every five minutes (actually, never do this).

Sexuality shouldn't be approached in fear, shame, or anxiety. Your students should know they have a safe space to talk about and seek wisdom for this sensitive, beautiful aspect of their humanity.

WHAT ABOUT BATHROOMS?

The bathroom question is more than just headline-making political controversy. Gender binary bathrooms—men's room and women's room—affect people of all gender identities, but they are particularly problematic for transgender and nonbinary youth. Being forced to use a bathroom that doesn't align with one's gender expression can be uncomfortable, stressful, dangerous, even traumatic. Some numbers to consider:

75% of transgender students feel unsafe at school because of their gender expression.

More than 63% of transgender students reported avoiding bathrooms.

51% **51% of trans youth can never use the restrooms or locker rooms that match their gender identity.**
Human Rights Campaign

When people feel unsafe in the bathroom, they don't go. Trans and nonbinary people have higher rates of urinary tract infections, and 31 percent have reported avoiding food and drink to reduce their need to use the bathroom.[31]

Schools, businesses, and public buildings are increasingly addressing the issue by providing bathroom space for all genders. It's not possible for churches to skate by without addressing the bathroom question. And it shouldn't be. Providing all-gender or gender-neutral restrooms is one of the most practical ways a church can create an LGBTQ+-welcoming space. It's a bright shining sign that says your church is thinking about how to care for queer people.

You might not have a transgender or nonbinary student currently in your congregation (that you know of). But don't wait to address the bathroom issue until a student comes out. Creating physical spaces that are safe and welcoming for all genders before a situation arises will help you avoid an awkward or hurtful situation. Transgender and nonbinary teenagers—and adults—need to know they are welcome in your church from the moment they walk in the door. Bathrooms are a great way to do this.

A COMMUNITY STATEMENT

Providing new facilities is a community-wide conversation and makes a community-wide statement of affirmation. Have the discussion with church staff and members now. Many schools and some churches are creating "Gender Support Plans" to proactively prepare for bathroom-related questions.[32] Your church can create something similar, where you address appropriate bathroom conduct and terms of use.

While you're sorting this out, you can still make moves to create a safe, gender-neutral bathroom. If possible, create at least one gender-neutral or all-gender restroom in your building. Even if you can only do this during youth events, you'll go a long way toward showing your queer students that their needs matter. And you'll show your church that this doesn't have to be a fraught process. Just cover one of the bathroom signs with a piece of paper that says "All-Gender Bathroom," and you've already made a huge difference.

For a more permanent solution, the church can designate an existing single-stall or multiple-stall facility as an all-gender bathroom. If you need help convincing the rest of the staff, remember that these facilities help everyone. In addition to your queer individuals, families with young children, disabled or elderly people who might need assistance in the bathroom, and people who want more privacy for whatever reason will all thank you.

FACING THE "WHAT IFS"

Your decision to create gender-inclusive bathrooms might be met with fear and resistance from parents, staff, students, or other members of the congregation. Though we can't anticipate every possible response to this change, there's a chance you'll be asked questions like these:

"What if my child doesn't feel comfortable with a transgender person in their bathroom?"

> Short answer: Ask them why, and calm their fears
> about queer youth with all you've learned in this book.

"What if someone pretends to be transgender and uses the other bathroom to be creepy?"

> Short answer: There is no data to suggest that this
> happens. It's just not a real threat.

"Why can't a transgender person just use a private bathroom?"

> Short answer: Forcing queer people into isolation is
> harmful and inappropriate.

"Why are we showing special treatment for just one person?"

> Short answer: Every person, literally *everyone*, should
> be able to pee without fear.

Don't be quick to assume that nay-sayers are prejudiced, homophobic bullies. They might be concerned parents who have simply never met a transgender person and don't really know what that means. Their uncertainty might cause them to fear the worst-case scenario. When communicating your decision to include all-gender restrooms, clearly explain your church's policy. Reassure parents that the safety and comfort of every student in your youth group is at the heart of your actions.

Creating an atmosphere where every gender identity and expression is welcome doesn't just benefit one person; it's a blessing to the entire group. If your reassurances aren't sufficient, refer people to Transgender Students and School Bathrooms: FAQ at genderspectrum.org, which offers great answers to frequently asked questions about trans people and bathrooms.

A FINAL THOUGHT

Unfortunately, some churches will refuse to budge on the bathroom issue. If your church is unwilling to accommodate a transgender or nonbinary student, it's up to you to let your student know that your church might not be a safe space for them.

If your church isn't willing to accept a student, be honest with them about it, and point them to another church or faith community that will. Finding a safe space for a young person is a bigger priority than retention.

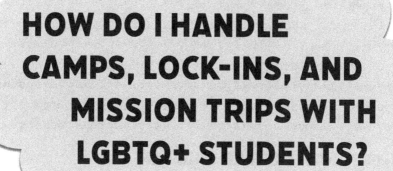

HOW DO I HANDLE CAMPS, LOCK-INS, AND MISSION TRIPS WITH LGBTQ+ STUDENTS?

Like it or not, the mountaintop moments of youth ministry often come during mission trips, backpacking excursions, outdoor ministry adventures, and lock-ins. These events provide opportunities for students to grow in faith, learn new skills, and test the limits of their regular routines.

NOT ALL FUN AND GAMES

Outings like these can generate loads of anxiety and fear for LGBTQ+ students. Most often, their concerns have to do with sleeping and showering arrangements. Whether you're in tents, cabins, hotel rooms, or church classrooms, it's common practice for sleeping and bathroom arrangements to be made according to gender. For a gender nonconforming person, this can be a nightmare. Still, sleeping arrangements are probably the number-one logistics question youth leaders and parents have when it comes to creating inclusive policies.

So here's our advice:

Don't figure this out on your own. If you have a youth committee or board, get them together for the express purpose of creating sustainable practices and expectations. Include some parents and students you think will have helpful input. Ensure that there are adult LGBTQ+ voices in the mix. Creating policy with a group makes for a far more comprehensive and defensible process.

Center your policy on the needs of your LGBTQ+ students. They are the most likely to suffer from poorly thought-out arrangements, so consider their safety your top priority. As with many of these conversations, what works for your queer students will likely have positive ripples for your whole group, so don't worry that you're choosing sides or elevating one group's needs over others. Good policy is good for everyone.

THIS IS NOT A QUEER PROBLEM.

Don't view this as a problem to be solved. You've got an opportunity to undo some of the more problematic (for all young people) parts of youth trips—public showering, group sleeping arrangements, etc. So remember that your policy is about teenagers, in relationship to themselves, their bodies, and the rest of your group. If any teenager wants privacy when changing clothes or taking a shower, honor that and *make it happen*. With subtlety and discretion.

Queer teenagers aren't the only ones who might be uncomfortable with these aspects of group living. Creating an expectation of privacy allows all students to feel more at ease.

PUT IN THE WORK.

The physical space you're in will shape your options, so be open to finding spaces that allow you to do what you need to do. It may take a bit more work, but it will benefit all of your students. Not every camp demands that students be divided by gender—there might be some that give you total control over sleeping arrangements. Go there instead.

Maybe your mission trip can include homestays instead of having the whole group divided into a bunch of church classrooms. Ask about bathrooms and showers. Ask about beds and changing areas. Throw some hypotheticals at your hosts and see what ideas they might have for adapting the space to fit your needs. We know of a camp for queer teenagers that lets campers choose their own cabins rather than assigning them; this has created zero issues. Or consider allowing students to sleep in one big room. Establish several feet of distance on each side of a sleeping bag to allow all students to sleep and move comfortably. Scatter adults throughout the room to make sure everyone is safe and comfortable.

In a setting that's a mix of queer and straight/cis students, allowing queer students to be with their friends, peers, and close supporters goes a long way toward helping them feel safe. Just because you've always gone somewhere or done things one way doesn't mean those things can't be reconsidered.

Be sure to communicate your new policies and practices clearly to staff, parents, and students. When you do, don't suggest you are making these changes because of the needs of a single student. Let people know these are changes that allow all students to feel safe and included. There might be pushback, especially regarding sleeping arrangements. Refer back to your process and the values you hold as a group, then frame your response as an outgrowth of these values.

Don't allow any predatory narratives to seep into your conversations around these changes. LGBTQ+ people are not predators, and anyone who implies or states that they are is wrong. Still, some parents, volunteers, or other students might see them that way. Remember, the statistics tell us that queer students are far more likely to be preyed upon, harassed, and harmed than their straight counterparts.

GET INTO THE DETAILS.

Look over permission slips and registration forms. Review flyers and invitations. Are they enforcing gender binary options—that is, asking individuals to mark whether they are male or female? If you're in charge of these forms, include a third option where students can write their gender identity and list any preferences for housing. This also helps you take the lead in talking to your LGBTQ+ students and their parents about their sleeping and showering preferences.

Ask, "What do you need to feel safe and comfortable?" Then tell them specifically how you're going to make that work. You might not be able to accommodate all of their requests, but it's important to ask for their input and do everything you can to address it. They need to hear that you consider it a privilege to be in their lives and that you want them to have a full and safe experience.

A FINAL THOUGHT

If, for any reason, you cannot accommodate your LGBTQ+ students on this event—which means they'll have to "tough it out" or just not participate—you probably shouldn't have it. If you have it, we're right back where we were with the bathroom question: it's up to you to let your student know that your church might not be a safe space for them.

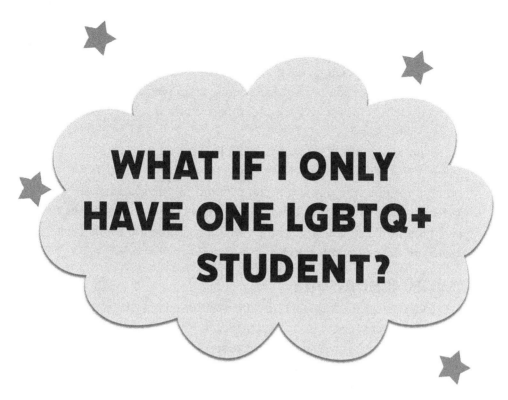

WHAT IF I ONLY HAVE ONE LGBTQ+ STUDENT?

You might know of only one queer student in your group, but don't assume they're the only one. You may have students who are not yet out, or you may have students who do not yet know they are LGBTQ+.

It's never safe to assume how many queer students you have until they let you know. It doesn't matter if there are five LGBTQ+ teenagers in your community or one or zero. Establishing a culture of acceptance is a good ministry practice, period. Look back at the section on creating safe spaces for ideas on how to do this.

THE BURDEN OF BEING THE ONLY ONE

Being the only queer person in any community can be very difficult. It's easy to become tokenized, or to be the "gay friend" to the straight/cis students. Some leaders pat themselves on the back for putting their welcoming values into action, and then let their concern for that person—or for other queer people—slide. (This is a big problem. Don't do it.)

At the same time, having one LGBTQ+ student who is out—even if it's just to you—gives you the chance to create a true connection with your student. You can set aside time to speak with the student about how they want to operate in the group. Do they have thoughts about the physical setup of the youth room, bathrooms, or sleeping arrangements on a trip? Do they want to come out to others? How can you support them in that process?

You and your student can walk through joys and questions and concerns they're now facing in a way that feels intentional and safe for both of you. Offer your unwavering support and encouragement, no matter what they want to do. Being the first openly queer person in the youth group will be hard, but together, you can pave the way for the next person and the next and the next.

RECOMMENDATIONS

Help your student think through situations and scenarios they might encounter as a participant in youth activities. Try to anticipate questions other students might have, uncomfortable spaces your student might encounter, parental concerns, and other ways your queer student's experience might play out in the group. Be ready to do the heavy lifting even as you work with your student. It helps them, which is the primary concern, but it also helps you understand what those concerns are and how to prepare for them with the group.

Be sure the burden of helping your group become more inclusive doesn't fall on your student or even entirely on you. Bring in a guest speaker, watch a video or movie about queer teenagers, or visit an organization that focuses on the needs of the LGBTQ+ community.

A FINAL THOUGHT

Don't underestimate your youth. They're likely more familiar with queer people and queer life than you are. Let them teach you about their interactions with LGBTQ+ people and culture. LGBTQ+ inclusiveness will likely be a bigger challenge with parents and other adults in the congregation. Empower all the youth to be advocates for queer youth everywhere.

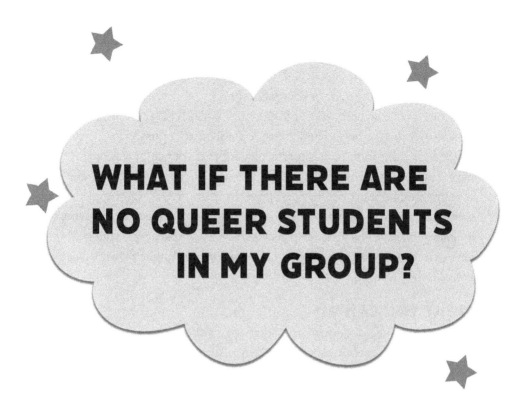

WHAT IF THERE ARE NO QUEER STUDENTS IN MY GROUP?

To be clear, you might not think there are any LGBTQ+ youth in your group, but the odds are you're mistaken. And assuming otherwise is naïve.

20% of 18- to 34-year-olds identify as LGBTQ+.

12% of 18- to 34-year-olds identify as trans or gender nonconforming.

GLAAD/Harris

These numbers represent a significant increase in people coming out as LGBTQ+. There are more young people identifying as queer in this generation than in any other in the past, and there's no evidence that will change.

So. The chances are pretty high that an LGBTQ+ teenager has been, is currently, or will be part of your youth group.

If one in five eighteen-year-olds identify as LGBTQ+, you might wonder why you've never had one come through your group.

Consider this useful but imperfect analogy: If your church doesn't have a ramp, not many people in wheelchairs will come to your church. If your church doesn't publicly and privately affirm LGBTQ+ people, you probably won't have any queer people show up (at least not any who are out to you). If you aren't actively creating a safe space for a young person to express their identity and orientation, they probably won't. Instead, they'll stay closeted or just leave.

WHAT YOU CAN DO

All churches, including open and affirming congregations, have room to grow in their acceptance and inclusion of LGBTQ+ people. Whether your church is affirming or still trying to figure out where they stand, you can initiate conversation with church leadership around some of these questions:

- ✦ What is our church's theology on affirming LGBTQ+ people?

- ✦ How is this theology being communicated? Have we been explicit that LGBTQ+ people are welcome and will be supported?

- ✦ Do our policies around involvement, marriage, volunteering, receiving communion, and other means of participation match our stated position?

- ✦ Who is represented in our church staff and volunteers? Do we have queer adults in leadership?

- ✦ Can same-sex couples get married in our church? If not, what do we tell them?

- ✦ What are people in our church hearing about LGBTQ+ people in our sermons, adult forums, youth groups, and Sunday school?

* How do we respond to bullying or acts of exclusion or bigotry from church members—adults and kids alike? Are we calling things out immediately or allowing microaggressions to slip by?

* Are we using gender-exclusive language and teaching resources in all education and discipleship settings?

* What about our physical space? Are the bathrooms, signs, symbols, and classrooms welcoming to LGBTQ+ people? Will they see themselves represented in the artwork, music, and books we use and promote?

You might not have much input on the core values, or even the vibe, of your church. But you are in a unique position to advocate for changes that will enrich the whole church by making space for people who have been left out for far too long. Social change often starts with young people, and you have the privilege of leading that change.

RECOMMENDATIONS

Start now . . .

For your LGBTQ+ students

If you want to encourage the LGBTQ+ teenagers who are or will be in your youth group, start creating a welcoming space now. If you're waiting to make your church a welcoming space until an LGBTQ+ person comes out, you risk being too late for those in your midst now.

For all your students

If you want your non-LGBTQ+ students to be welcoming to their LGBTQ+ peers, start teaching them now. Chances are, many of your students already know and interact with many LGBTQ+ friends at school or in extracurricular activities. Ask them why they think their queer friends don't feel comfortable in church. Listen to their ideas on how to change this.

For yourself
If you want to be a safe and trusted support for an LGBTQ+ teenager, say so publicly and act on your intentions now. Be a leader in affirming LGBTQ+ people in your church. Be an advocate on social media and in your local community. Preach against bullying, and speak out against misinformation and harmful stereotypes. Build a reputation for being a group where queer teenagers will find a home.

A FINAL THOUGHT

Even if you can't do much to change your church environment, engaging in these conversations and doing what you can shows your students that queer issues are important to you. And you're actively helping all of your students become agents of grace, care, and kindness in and outside of youth group. Even if no one comes out to you, it's important for you to show any closeted students that your faith community is trying their best to be welcoming and affirming. Remember that just because a young person doesn't come out in their teens, that doesn't mean they never will. They might come out in a year or a decade from now. But they'll remember the impact and impression your church is making now.

Troy, 21:

> I attend an ELCA congregation in Salt Lake City. It's a warm, tight community that says it welcomes anyone and everyone. It's a community I've been a part of for years, and one I'm intimately connected to in more ways all the time. It's also the last place I came out.

> It's not that I didn't want to come out at church. Being closeted, hiding that part of myself, was deeply painful. Putting on a brave face and saying all was well when I was actually suicidally depressed. Every time I held back my

truth, told a half-lie, or shrugged off a question about my dating life, it hurt. I wanted to say something, I wanted to be myself, but I didn't feel like I could.

I didn't want to face all the stereotypes and associations and misconceptions that go with being gay. If I came out of the closet, so would some of my shameful skeletons. I was worried coming out would mean admitting that I've thought about sexuality, which, gay or not, was something I was deeply ashamed of. I didn't want to jeopardize my future in ministry or my place in the community. And so, burdened by expectations and feeling trapped, I hid.

When I finally came out at church, it was in a council meeting. We were discussing our cookie-cutter welcome statement, and the feeling I got from the room was "patting ourselves on the back." "Of course we welcome everyone! It's who we are!" I spoke up with something I'd wanted to say for years:

"Let me say, as a gay person, I don't feel welcome here. There's a reason I've never come out."

Since then, my congregation has changed, and I have too. I'm much more content as a member of the community now that I can be my authentic self. There's a sense of love and welcome I've never felt before. And I think a part of that is because I spoke up. I'm happier at church now than I have been in a long time. I'm still a volunteer and a candidate for ministry. The congregation I nearly left for not welcoming me feels radically different now from how it did before. I've gotten past the expectations and learned to be myself at church—I'm different, but in a good way. And as it turned out, God had a plan to use the authentic me in my congregation to teach, to lead, and to help make a welcoming place for others.

HOW DO I RECOGNIZE AND CONFRONT RELIGIOUS ABUSE?

As people of faith, we believe our relationship with God and efforts at growing in God's love should influence our language, actions, and beliefs. But as you know, religion has not always followed this model. Too often, religion has been used to perpetuate hate and greed, deceive devoted followers, even justify genocide. When religion is used to bring harm to an individual or group, it is, quite simply, religious and spiritual abuse.

Unfortunately, religious abuse isn't limited to the past. In the last few decades, LGBTQ+ people have been targets of tremendous religious bigotry and abuse. Consider that while involvement in religion and a faith community reduces the risk of suicide in most adults, a recent study from the *American Journal of Preventive Medicine* found that LGBTQ+ people who placed a high importance on religion were *38% more likely* to commit suicide.

 57% of LGBTQ+ youth say that churches or places of worship in their community are not accepting.

 68% of LGBTQ+ youth say they hear negative messages about being LGBTQ+ from religious leaders.

Human Rights Campaign

This is a deeply disturbing reality that every church leader has to confront. It transcends theological disputes and biblical interpretation. Religious abuse in our churches literally puts lives at risk. Regardless of theology or denomination, we encourage you to examine your church's participation in or condoning of religious and spiritual abuse and to enact change to stop it from continuing.

WHAT DOES RELIGIOUS ABUSE LOOK LIKE?

Broadly speaking, religious abuse is when aspects of religion are used to devalue the way a person understands and appraises their worth. Religious abuse uses guilt, shame, manipulation, and fear as means of control. When it comes to LGBTQ+ people, religious abuse looks like efforts to demonize LGBTQ+ people for their identities and exclude them from full participation in faith communities.

Religious abuse shames from pulpits, inspires anger and fear, directs hatred at a person or group of people. Often, this abuse is done in the guise of love and right living. But it is simply abuse.

While this is obviously damaging to anyone who experiences it, messages that attach shame and guilt to a person's identity can be especially harmful to young people.

Religious abuse doesn't just happen at church. It can occur at home, at school, or in any interpersonal relationships in a queer teenager's life. Religious abuse can look and sound like many things:

- Derogatory language, prayers, or Scripture passages used intentionally to make someone feel shame or to control their behavior.

- Casting queer sexual orientations or gender identities as sinful.

- Conversion therapy, including pray-the-gay-away intervention. (see page 66).

- Teaching the "clobber" verses as the Bible's primary statement on sexuality.

- Shutting down questions or conversations about sexuality.

- Removal from positions of leadership or exclusion from groups at church because of an LGBTQ+ identity.

- Overtly anti-gay/trans/queer sermons, language, or practices.

- Mentions of LGBTQ+ people as sexually promiscuous, predatory, or mentally ill.

HOW TO RECOGNIZE THE EFFECTS OF RELIGIOUS ABUSE

If a teenager grew up in a context where religious abuse was common, they might not recognize the harm they've experienced or continue to experience. The pervasiveness of shame-based thinking and language in families and faith communities can be so deeply rooted in a teenager that they have internalized those messages and believe they have always been there. That belief and the self-loathing that comes with it can be very difficult to admit and overcome.

Now, we acknowledge (and you should do the same) that you won't be able to singlehandedly undo the false messages and bad theology queer teenagers have experienced. And you won't be able to undo the deep harm that can come from a lifetime of hearing that God hates your very identity. You can't save LGBTQ+ teenagers from the harm Christianity has done to them.

But you can learn to recognize the language of brokenness. And you can tell them, maybe for the first time in their lives, that it's wrong. And you can start the process of undoing the damage that's been done.

Here's what to listen for from LGBTQ+ youth:

- Prayers centered on shame and self-deprecation
- More conversations about guilt than about God's love and grace
- Doubts about God's love or acceptance
- Anger or bitterness toward the larger church or the congregation
- A big-guy-in-the-sky or puppet-master view of God rather than the sense of God as a loving presence
- Emphasis on good works or perfectionism as a way to earn God's grace
- Fear of talking to religious authority figures
- Blaming all personal problems on their sexual orientation or gender identity
- Attempts or hopes to change their identity
- Symptoms of anxiety and depression (see page 196)
- Internalized homophobia/transphobia

That's a lot to hold on to. Even students who are involved in loving, affirming churches will likely deal with the implications of such past messages for years to come. Still, as a spiritual leader in a queer teenager's life, you can present them with a grace-based approach to the Bible and the teachings of Jesus:

God is love, and those who abide in love abide in God,
and God abides in them.

—1 John 4:16

WHAT TO DO ABOUT IT

Religious abuse is sin, plain and simple. If you're seeking out some ideas of how to address this sinful behavior within your church, look no further than Matthew 18:15–20. Jesus indicates that a good starting place is a one-on-one conversation with the offending person. This might be difficult as a church leader. You might be entering into a conversation with a member of the church staff, a pastor, a deacon, an elder, or a member of the church council or board. Nevertheless, you are empowered by the Holy Spirit to speak on behalf of the victims of religious abuse.

Enter into this conversation with empathy and a willingness to have a dialogue. Let the person you're talking to know what you've observed and why you're concerned. Indicate your hope that the problematic behavior will change.

If your conversation proves unsuccessful, check back with Matthew 18. Jesus tells you to bring two others into the situation. In your case, this may be another youth leader, a parent of a queer student, or an LGBTQ+ ally within the congregation. These people are with you to offer support and to listen, but not to pile on or bully.

If you still aren't getting anywhere with the person, Jesus says to "tell it to the church." In this instance, you might want to start with the council or other leadership body before running an article in the church newsletter or posting your concerns broadly on social media. If you're able to handle this conversation with integrity and avoid meeting their abuse with abuse of your own, you'll have a greater chance of winning over the hearts and minds of the offending party.

If you still aren't able to convince the church leaders of your concern—maybe the offender *is* the church leader—Jesus indicates that the sinning member should be treated "as a Gentile and a tax collector." This is more complicated than it might seem. Lest you think this means Jesus is telling you to throw them out of the church, remember the way Jesus related to tax collectors and Gentiles: He remained in relationship with them and continued to teach and walk alongside them. But he didn't back down from speaking the truth. Neither should you.

Not every church is going to change their language or theology on LGBTQ+ issues. Your church might be one of them that doesn't. Be aware of and realistic about your church's stance on LGBTQ+ inclusion and how the student is internalizing that message.

Sometimes it's okay and even necessary to advise a teenager/ family to leave the church in favor of a more affirming congregation. Allowing—even encouraging—a student and their family to leave an unhealthy environment isn't giving up. Ultimately, by admitting that your church is not the best fit, you are making a student's safety and well-being your primary concern (as they should be). Before having this conversation, make sure you know of affirming denominations or churches in your area to recommend to a student and their family.

RECOMMENDATIONS

If you recognize religious/spiritual abuse occurring in your church, address it directly. Have learning campaigns to recognize the signs and harm of religious abuse. Start your LGBTQ+ learning campaign by reaching out to a queer religious or denominational organization—many are listed in the back of this book—and ask them for assistance in undertaking this challenge.

If religious abuse is coming from family/parents, speak with them about the harm they're doing to their teenager and how that will impact their ongoing parent/child relationship. Family acceptance is the number-one safeguard against the risks faced by LGBTQ+ teenagers. As a leader, you have an opportunity to speak truth and love into an entire family and break apart systems of religious oppression, one family at a time.

If you see religious abuse occurring in a situation that you have no influence over or that simply will not change, keep pouring into the young person stories of love, grace, and acceptance. This is who Jesus is. This is what the church is called to be. Affirm your student as wholly loved by you and by God. Remind them that they will not be in this circumstance forever. Offer them support until they can leave the unhealthy environment.

A FINAL THOUGHT

Religious abuse is powerful, and its effects are lasting. While language of guilt and shame certainly affects all members of a congregation, LGBTQ+ teenagers are at particular risk of being isolated and rejected by this kind of church culture. Though a person's harmful language and actions might not have bad intentions, they often result in pain and condemnation. We are called to create communities of love and inclusion, giving space and freedom for a young person to experience God individually and communally.

Let this truth be what your students hear and see from you and your staff. Eliminating religious abuse in our churches is essential to the spiritual, mental, and physical health of LGBTQ+ teenagers.

WHAT ABOUT BIGOTS IN THE CONGREGATION?

Bigots. Yep. We really are going to call people bigots. If that seems pretty harsh, well, maybe it is. And we'd recommend you avoid name-calling in your ongoing dialogue with people in your congregation. However, sometimes we have to call something what it is. Anyone who is intolerant of those who are different or who hold a different opinion is, by definition, a bigot.

> **bigot:** *noun*
> A person who has very strong, unreasonable beliefs or opinions about race, religion, or politics and who will not listen to or accept the opinions of anyone who disagrees
> *(Oxford)*

NOT IN MY CHURCH, THOUGH . . .

We hate to tell you, but: there are bigots in your church.

They don't all look the same, dress the same way, or vote for the same political candidates. In fact, they might be some of the nicest people you know. Churches are made up of people—well-intentioned, opinionated, hurting, imperfect people. Your church is no different.

Even in the most progressive churches, there will be people who are nonaffirming or who actively voice their bias against the LGBTQ+ community. Even if someone says they're affirming, they might be bigoted in their language or behavior. As a youth leader, you're in a position to gracefully call out and correct bigotry and prejudice.

REMEMBER GRACE

Bigotry and bias don't always stem from malicious intent. Often, bigotry comes from a place of ignorance. So root all your interactions in grace. Having patience and grace is essential in walking with someone from rejection to acceptance. Conversely, forcing an angry confrontation, especially with someone with whom you have no relationship, is only going to cause others to dig deeper into their own argument. So even as you're fighting bigotry, be sure to foster relationships among all members of your congregation.

This is yet another reason to make sure your LGBTQ+ students know they are valued and feel included in your youth group. This will help others see them as part of the congregation. And studies show that getting to know an LGBTQ+ person and carefully building a relationship with them can be the most powerful tool for breaking through their anti-queer prejudice and long-held assumptions.

What better context for this to occur than in church? Of course, you never want to force your students into a situation that tokenizes them, or that presents toxic or potentially harmful outcomes. But if your congregation sees your LGBTQ+ students being welcomed, embraced, and valued by your group, hopefully they will follow suit.

RECOMMENDATIONS

If you recognize bigotry in a volunteer:

★ Be clear about the behaviors you've witnessed or heard about that are unacceptable. Use your group covenant and core values as a benchmark for expected behavior.

- Pay attention to what's happening in the room. Look for words, attitudes, behaviors, and reactions that point to a bias against queer people. You might need to address these things in real time in front of the group, but ideally, you can pull your volunteer aside and talk to them privately about this problematic behavior.

- If your volunteer shows a willingness to learn and grow, put together a plan to help them do that. Connect them with resources; introduce them to queer adults who can share their stories and help build understanding and empathy for your LGBTQ+ students. Stay open to their questions or concerns, knowing that people need time to change.

- Be prepared for the possibility of your volunteer becoming angry or withdrawing from the group. This is regrettable, but if they're doing harm, they shouldn't be in a position of leadership with your students.

If anti-LGBTQ+ bigotry is present in the majority of your congregation:

- Communicate to your senior staff, elders, and anyone else in leadership that you intend to lead your youth ministry as an affirming space to the church.

- Be prepared for pushback. If you are welcoming LGBTQ+ teenagers in a nonaffirming church, you'll likely make people angry.

- Don't make individual students the focus of a theological argument among adults. Don't use individuals or their stories, especially without their knowledge or consent, as ammunition.

- Admit and lament that your church, and probably your youth group, might not be a safe space for LGBTQ+ teenagers.

- Communicate the reality of the congregation's attitudes to the LGBTQ+ students so they can make choices about their ongoing participation in the church.

If bigotry comes from a single voice or a few voices:

★ Talk to the person about what you're seeing, why it's harmful, and what can be done.

★ Educate people about the harm bigotry can do, even if it's "well-intentioned."

★ Elicit help from other adults who know the person.

★ Keep other trusted leaders in the loop on your concerns and conversations.

★ Don't "out" this person or people to your students. 1) This isn't their problem to solve, and 2) you don't know what kind of relationship or connections your students might have with this person.

★ Pray for changed hearts and healed relationships in your church.

A FINAL THOUGHT

Bigotry doesn't just harm the people it's aimed at. It affects everyone in your congregation and sets a tone for the culture of your church. Confronting bigotry presents an opportunity for your students to learn how to navigate conflict in a Christlike way. Show them how to do this without creating sides in a congregational fight.

Jo, 21:

> It's hard to be in an environment where people you respect and care for are so discriminatory—where you know that if they found out that one thing about you, none of the rest of you would matter. I used to think, "They're such a nice person, even if they are homophobic." And something I learned with time is that, no, they're not a nice person. People who hate someone else because they're different are not nice people. And they are not people you need to have in your life.

HOW CAN I CREATE A CULTURE OF AFFIRMATION IN MY CHURCH?

One of your responsibilities, even though it's probably not in your job description, is to be a culture creator. You're likely already doing this in your youth ministry. The games you play, the curriculum you use, the inside jokes you laugh at, the way you speak about God, and the kind of events you plan are all ways you are creating a particular culture in your ministry.

Your broader congregation has a culture too. Church members might not always be able to articulate what this culture is, but most people will know how it makes them feel.

Anyone who has ever stepped into a new church for the first time knows that your spidey senses kick in and you can tell pretty quickly whether this is a place for you or not. That sense is turned up to eleven for people who have not traditionally been welcomed or embraced by the church—i.e., queer people. A queer person—be it an adult or a teenager—can tell pretty quickly whether your church culture is inclusive and affirming for them. So if you want to make sure your church is that kind of place, you might need to push for some changes.

LISTEN!

The best place to start is to listen to queer people—those in your community and those who can identify what affirmation and inclusion have looked like in other places. For example:

Beth, 21:

> I have been incredibly lucky to have parents and friends who are incredible allies of the LGBTQ+ community. My church was a different story. My mother is the senior pastor of our church, and after I came out to her at age 15, she began to work and make our church a place which welcomes, accepts, and celebrates the LGBTQ+ community. Many church members left our church, fearing change and thinking that people who are queer are going to hell. These people were physically and financially replaced in about two years with a myriad of gay couples who had finally found a place to belong. I now feel safe being at my church, and I know my church family supports me in my sexuality AND spirituality.

Trystan, 20:

> I have been out at church for a little over a year now. Honestly, coming out as nonbinary and queer at church was an extremely anxiety-provoking experience. I was worried about how people would react, and whether they would use the name and pronouns I asked them to use. I chose to make a coming out post on Facebook, because I am friends with everyone I socialize with at church on there, and I decided it would be easier than trying to tell everyone individually in person. My parents, pastors, and closest friends at church already knew about how I identified, and it was helpful knowing I had their support going into this. My church family has always been amazing at showing me unconditional love and support, and this instance was no different. Some commented on the Facebook post in support of me. Many welcomed me at church the next Sunday with my chosen name and

pronouns. I felt a huge sense of relief, like I was finally able to be my full self around those I loved and worshipped with. This past June, after getting my name legally changed to my chosen name, I had a renaming service at my church. My pastors led liturgy that recognized my birth name, my chosen name and pronouns, and celebrated my identity in my chosen name. There was a song rewritten by a friend of mine, a remembering of baptism and a prayer of blessing all to celebrate this milestone in my journey. Many members of my church family attended, as well as friends from elsewhere. Whether it is a day of celebration of my identity, or a normal day, I always feel the love and support of my church family.

RECOMMENDATIONS

Do an audit of your physical space. What overt and covert messages are being communicated in the artwork, bulletin boards, posters, signage? Are the words gendered? Do all the people in pictures and images look alike? Make a list of any items that might express narrow, unwelcoming, or exclusionary attitudes within the congregation.

Make changes, but keep it small at first. Make minor, but significant, changes to the troublesome items on your list. In doing so, you're letting your community know that words and images matter. Avoid trying to change your church culture with one big, bold action. Hanging a twenty-five foot rainbow flag outside your church isn't going to win over as many people as you think, and you risk alienating people who might need a little time to change their thinking.

You can do more harm than good if the culture of your church doesn't reflect the message of affirmation and love that you're trying to create. If you're going to say everyone is welcome, make sure that's actually true.

WHAT ARE MY REPORTING/SHARING RESPONSIBILITIES?

Having a student come out to you can raise questions around your responsibility to report or share information with parents, guardians, church staff, and other adults. If a young person comes out to you, it's because they trust you with their privacy and their process. To the best of your ability, it's imperative that you don't break this trust.

Outing someone takes away their ability to shape their own story and could possibly put the young person in danger. It's crucial to avoid any assumptions about how anyone else will respond to news that their child is queer. Often, a young queer person's parents are among the harmful people in their life.

PROTECT, DON'T OUT

When a student discloses their sexual orientation or gender identity to you, you are under no legal obligation to share this with others. Unless your church has a policy requiring you to do this (hopefully they don't; if they do, work to change it), you should share no more than what your student gives you permission to share. Let them dictate how to proceed in their process of coming out.

However, if your student gives you any sign of being in physical danger (in an abusive relationship or contemplating self-harm or suicide), you are legally obligated to report this to the proper authorities—not just within the church, but legal authorities as well. Check the mandatory-reporter guidelines in your state for some guidance here (a quick online search will lead you to them). Your congregation's child safety policy might have more specific language about procedures if a person is at risk.

You'll also want to set up clear expectations with parents, volunteers, and other church staff so they know how you're going to handle confidential conversations with your students. This is just good practice for youth leaders, regardless of whether you have an out LGBTQ+ student. Review these expectations at the beginning of every program year so everyone is on board and knows what your boundaries are.

The way you share—or don't share—information will depend on who you're sharing, or not sharing, it with. So think about how you'll communicate with other adults well before you need to.

WITH PARENTS

* Never out a young person to their parents. Even if they are in physical danger, speak about the concerning behavior or circumstance without informing them of their child's LGBTQ+ identity. You don't have all the details about why the parents don't know.

* Ask a young person if they would like you to be a mediator between them and their parents when they do come out or have other concerns their parents need to know about. Be prepared to moderate these conversations or bring in someone else who can do that work. You can still be present, but know your limits when it comes to mediating difficult family situations.

* If the student is out at home, communicate your sharing process early and often with your queer student and their parents. Set a standard of confidentiality for the youth and openness with parents, then stick to it.

WITH CHURCH STAFF

- ✦ You are more than likely a mandated reporter, but take a look at your church's policy on reporting. Does it extend to your adult volunteers? Does it allow you to make judgment calls? If it does, we strongly recommend erring on the side of a student's safety, not your reputation. What other staff people at the church need to be notified of a safety concern?

- ✦ What are your senior pastor's expectations of disclosure among church staff? If you don't know, or if you think they need to change, schedule a time to talk through the pastor's expectations and yours. If you need to, write down what you agree to do when a student comes out. You and the pastor could easily get caught in a difficult family dynamic, and you'll want to be sure you have agreed on your approach well before that happens.

- ✦ Stick to your own policy. Depending on your position at the church, you might feel pressured to reveal information in order to keep your job or to avoid making waves with other staff. Remember that your most important role is to protect your students from harm. If you're asked to choose a side, choose your student.

WITH VOLUNTEERS

- ✦ Don't assume that because a young person came out to you, they want every youth group volunteer to know. Be clear with your student that you won't tell anyone else unless they want you to or you have a concern about their safety.

- ✦ Be very careful about hinting at what you know about a student with your volunteers. Avoid the old "prayer-as-gossip" trap and any other subtle signals that you have information about a student that they don't.

★ As you engage your volunteers in making the kinds of culture and space changes discussed in this book, be clear that it's the right thing to do. Don't tie these changes to the identity of your queer student.

RECOMMENDATIONS

We've already said it, but it bears repeating: You should never out anyone to anyone. Unless you absolutely must, keep this information to yourself. You've been given a great gift; act accordingly.

Report what must be reported, but only to those required. Some issues call for mandated reporting but not parental notification. Some call for parental notification but not mandated reporting. Be aware of what the particular situation demands.

You might need to inform the family of physical risks or dangers their teenager might be facing—self-harm, running away, drug or alcohol abuse. You can safely inform a family of these risks without outing their child. Be sure to tell your student about what you will and will not disclose from the very beginning of your conversations.

If a young person is in danger of any kind and you have to report something, do what is required, but keep the young person's well-being and interests first. The child welfare system can be slow, hard, and even dangerous. As soon as a young person enters official care (be it foster care, hospitalization, or in-patient treatment), they are often abandoned by or isolated from their community, family, and church leaders.

That's not a reason to not report concerns about abuse or self-harm. But if your report results in institutionalization of any kind, find ways to continue to be an affirming, stable presence in your student's life. Be their advocate. Help them find the resources they need to stay safe—a social worker, a therapist, a guardian ad litem (basically, a lawyer who works with minors). Let them know you do not intend to leave them alone and are committed to putting their interests first.

A FINAL THOUGHT

When a young person discloses something about their identity or situation to you, your job is to be an ally and an advocate. Don't add drama to the situation. You're not keeping a secret; you're a part of a young person's growth and identity formation. Ask the young person how they would like you to proceed after they come out. Respect their desire for privacy, and never assume that the parents know. Don't project what you would want to know as a parent or how your child would act in the situation. Be supportive, helpful, and safe. Always act with integrity, even when withholding information.

WHAT CAN I TELL THE PARENTS?

Youth ministry is a partnership between the church and home. Parents play an important role in their child's faith formation, and kids who pray at home with their parents are more likely to stay connected to the church into adulthood than kids who pray alone. People are often surprised to learn that parents, not pastors or youth leaders, are the primary spiritual influencer for young people. But parents don't just cover the faith front at home. Youth leaders also lean on parents for help with activities at church. Parents provide transportation for retreats, coordinate church fundraisers, chaperone trips, and lead confirmation small groups. Youth leaders lean on parents to make their jobs easier, and vice versa.

The relationship between parents and youth leaders is unique and special, just like your relationship with their teenagers. And that makes it complicated to hold on to confidential information. It might feel gross at times, but you might need to keep things from parents, especially if a queer kid comes out to you and they're not ready to tell their parents.

When an LGBTQ+ person comes out, it is usually a thoughtful, intentional decision on their part to share information with certain people. When they do, there's an expectation of trust. It's imperative that you not break that trust without a very, *very*, VERY good reason.

WHAT IS OUTING?

The Human Rights Campaign defines *outing* as an act that reveals an LGBTQ+ person's sexual orientation or gender identity without their consent.

Outing someone takes away their story, their privacy, their process, and their power. If a young person is coming out to you and not to their parents, trust that they know what they're doing. Never assume parents will be accepting when it comes to their child's gender identity or sexual orientation.

Be aware that just because a teenager isn't telling their parents right now doesn't mean it'll be that way forever. And it doesn't necessarily mean they're afraid they'll be rejected. Sometimes they just aren't ready for the conversations and the questions that will come. Even the most affirming parents are likely to have questions and feel loss when their child comes out. So give them time. Be a non-anxious presence in their lives. Let your student dictate the terms for the time being.

A FINAL THOUGHT

When you feel you need to disclose information to another adult, do so in a calm, even-handed manner. Avoid projecting with statements like "I've known this for a while," or "I'm hesitant to trust you with this information." This isn't a contest or a way to passive-aggressively shame parents. Be supportive and helpful to both your student and their family. Lead with kindness and compassion.

WHAT IF MY QUEER STUDENT ISN'T SAFE AT HOME?

Family disapproval over the revelation of a child's LGBTQ+ identity is, sadly, the norm. Let's take a look at the numbers:

67% of LGBTQ+ youth hear their families make negative comments about LGBTQ+ people.

Almost half of LGBTQ+ youth who are out to their parents say their families have a negative response to their being LGBTQ+.

Only 24% of LGBTQ+ youth can "definitely" be themselves at home.

36%	QUEER
33%	LESBIAN AND GAY
27%	BISEXUAL

36% of queer youth, 33% of lesbian and gay youth, and 27% of bisexual youth report that their families are "very accepting."

 1 in 4 LGBTQ+ youth have families who show support for them by getting involved in the larger LGTBQ and ally community.

Human Rights Campaign

If you discover that a teenager is experiencing family disapproval over their LGBTQ+ identity, you might find yourself caught in the middle and feel compelled to avoid taking sides. And while you don't want to intentionally alienate families, your primary responsibility is to advocate for your student's safety and well-being.

So, please, take your queer kid's side.

ALL REJECTION IS NOT EQUAL

Your first step in mediating between parents/guardians and your students is to evaluate the degree to which the family disapproves:

- ✦ Is the family struggling to accept their teenager's LGBTQ+ identity?
- ✦ Are they actively trying to change the identity of their teenager?
- ✦ Is there a threat of physical or emotional violence?
- ✦ Are they threatening to or actively removing their teenager from the house?

Differing levels of disapproval will require differing levels of engagement from you as a leader.

FAILURE TO ACCEPT:

If a family is struggling to accept their teenager's identity, your role might be to allow them space to process or even grieve. You can point them to resources like PFLAG, which provides support to parents of queer children or to a family counselor who specializes in working with queer teenagers. Often, parents who were initially uncomfortable with their child's identity come to accept it with time and information.

ATTEMPT TO CHANGE:

If a family is actively trying to change their teenager's identity, meet with them to learn more about the reasons behind their actions, and be sure to educate them on the very real dangers presented by conversion therapy.

They might have outdated and even dangerous ideas about why their teenager is queer or believe being queer is a choice. Make sure they know that not only will conversion therapy fail, but it risks creating lasting, even permanent rifts in their relationship with their child. You don't need to scare the family, but someone must make them aware of the unintended consequences that can come from their lack of acceptance.

ABUSIVE OR VIOLENT:

If a family is emotionally or physically abusive or threatening to kick their child out of the home, you need to be more direct with your intervention. Be very clear about the dangers they are putting their child in by refusing to accept them. Don't hesitate to enlist the help of other church leaders, mental health professionals, or a therapist to advocate on behalf of the teenager who is being mistreated by their parents.

You might feel out of place inserting yourself into a family's affairs. It's good to be sensitive to the complexity of family systems. It's also good to know you're in a unique position to be a safe space for a teenager and a resource for their entire family.

RECOMMENDATIONS

When working with families:

* ★ Have resources on hand to share with families struggling with their teenager's LGBTQ+ identity.

* ★ Be sensitive. Don't pretend to know or understand the whole story of your student, their family relationships, or the emotions involved.

* ★ Know and be able to articulate your church's boundaries, practices, and expectations of you and your staff.

* ★ Know when you are out of your depth and need to lean on trained moderators, counselors, or social workers who are better equipped to succeed on behalf of LGBTQ+ young people.

* ★ Advocate against conversion therapy to any family who suggests it. Explain why it's dangerous and doesn't work.

A FINAL THOUGHT

There's no question that these conversations can put you in an awkward, even confrontational situation. This is seriously hard work, and no one wants to get caught in the middle of a fraught family situation. It will be crucial for you to know yourself and where you can and can't be effective in helping families navigate this process. And make sure to have a support system of your own. You will be a better advocate and a better leader if you are caring for your own physical, emotional, and spiritual needs.

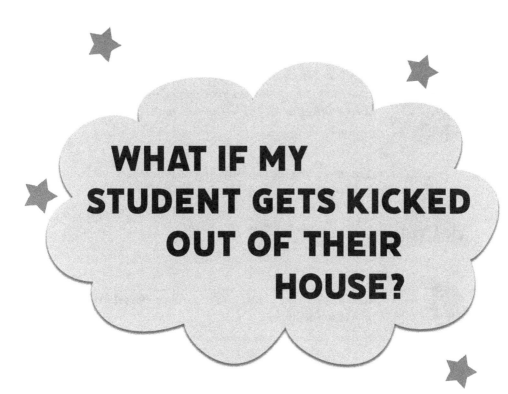

WHAT IF MY STUDENT GETS KICKED OUT OF THEIR HOUSE?

From the laws of Moses to the Psalms and the prophets and even the book of James, the Bible has a lot to say about the way people of faith should treat outsiders, orphans, and other people who are rejected and oppressed. Teenagers who are kicked out of their house or are disowned by their parents essentially function as orphans. Our faith obligates us to see that their basic needs are provided for.

THE DATA

LGBTQ+ teenagers are much more likely to experience homelessness or foster care than their heterosexual peers. Most often, this is because of family rejection and a lack of acceptance from peers:

LGBTQ+ teenagers are 120% more likely to experience homelessness compared to teenagers who identify as heterosexual and cisgender.

Human Rights Campaign

LGBTQ+ teenagers comprise up to 40% of the total unaccompanied homeless youth population, even though they make up 5–10% of the overall youth population.
Human Rights Campaign

 Teenagers who are experiencing homelessness are at an increased risk for sexual abuse and exploitation, chemical and alcohol dependency, social stigma, and discrimination.
Human Rights Campaign

 62% of LGBTQ+ youth who experience homelessness will attempt suicide.
National Coalition for the Homeless

These statistics are alarming.

Adolescence is a crucial period of social, psychological, educational, and physical development. Experiencing homelessness at any point during these years puts teenagers at a higher risk of missing out on key opportunities for growth and maturity toward a healthy, productive adulthood.[33] If you think anyone in your youth group is at risk of homelessness, take immediate action.

EARLY INTERVENTION

There are usually warning signs before an LGBTQ+ teenager is kicked out of the house. Be watchful for signs that rejection or abuse may be happening—such as increased exhaustion, refusal to go home, or verbal clues that things are bad at home—and try to intervene before they are kicked out.

Invite parents/guardians into conversations about the well-being of their child. Listen to their concerns while letting them know of the risks their child will face if they are kicked out. Help them understand that this is not a loving or effective way to force a child to reject their identity.

Here's a strategy if things are very dire: One way to avoid homelessness is a negotiated, short-term arrangement to "give each other space." Allowing the teenager to stay with a friend or family member for an agreed-upon amount of time—be it a weekend or a month—can allow parents needed time to process together, pray, and let their emotions cool, all with the understanding that no firm decisions have been made.

Even this solution, though, is best avoided. Moving in with a friend or relative can put a teenager in a precarious position legally. Be prepared to advocate for and to rally additional advocates for your student, be it with the family, with lawyers, or in court.

IF THEY GET KICKED OUT

If your student asks for help after getting forced out of their home, assist in finding a temporary housing situation. Staying with friends, extended family, or a known church family that understands the situation and consents to allowing them to stay can alleviate an immediate crisis and give the family time to work through this situation.

Once a teenager is kicked out, many factors make it difficult for them to be reinstated in safe housing. This is why it's crucial for you to do what you can to stop homelessness from occurring *before* a situation occurs.

It's also a very good idea to build a network of families who are safe and willing to house a potentially at-risk student, queer or nonqueer. Become familiar with community resources, shelters, and government agencies that deal with youth homelessness. These should be considered a last resort, but you need to know what the options are in your community.

AGE MATTERS

The ramifications of kicking a child out of the home are extreme at any age. But consider how old the student is in each situation. A middle-schooler facing family rejection is a different situation than a high-school senior, looking toward graduation.

There's never an acceptable time, ever, to reject an LGBTQ+ family member. But it's possible to argue for a solution in some cases—"Just wait until graduation" could convince a family with a seventeen-year-old—that won't work in all cases.

RECOMMENDATIONS

If a teenager is still at home and facing the prospect of homelessness:

* Learn to recognize the signs of family rejection: explosive family arguments, physical abuse, anxiety and depression, lack of concentration, shutting down when talking about family.

* Bring in influential support systems—pastors, school administrators, family counselors, or social workers—to help the family work their way through this situation.

* Help parents find support with other families of queer children or through organizations like PFLAG.

* Make parents aware of the danger they are putting their child in by forcing homelessness. Help them understand that no matter how they feel about their child's sexuality or gender identity, they put their teenager at tremendous risk by kicking them out.

* Help your student formulate a plan in case they have to leave home. Investigate short-term solutions (temporary housing with friends or in a shelter) and long-term solutions (returning home or finding independent housing elsewhere).

If a teenager has already been kicked out:

* Establish communication and a support system with your student. Make sure you know how to reach them and vice versa.

* Point them to the homelessness resources in your community. Drive them to a shelter if you have to. Help them get a social worker or other community advocate who can help them navigate the system. Be aware that not every organization is safe for LGBTQ+ teenagers, especially trans teenagers. Make sure you have identified safe resources that are designed for LGBTQ+ people.

- Don't catastrophize this. Homelessness doesn't have to be permanent. It's doesn't have to be the end of a teenager's hope for a good life. Do what you can to help your student's regular routines stay as normal as possible—going to school, coming to youth activities, connecting with friends.

- Recognize how this affects your youth group, and talk about it in a boundary-respecting way.

- Pray for the families and teenagers. If you're praying with them, be very aware of your language. Do not passively reveal sentiments or opinions.

A FINAL THOUGHT

As difficult as it might be to say no, do not take a student into your own home or let other adult volunteers do so. As church staff, you have to establish healthy boundaries. You cannot be all things to all people. By taking in a student, you will likely break down the relationship you have with their parents and put your chances of fostering reconciliation and discussion between parents and child at risk.

WHAT ELSE DO I NEED TO KNOW?

There's no job quite like working with youth, but you already know that. You have to be a lot of things to a lot of different people. The work you do asks you to be a teacher, a friend, a comedian, a therapist, a pastor, a disciplinarian, a volunteer coordinator, a travel agent, a social worker, a coach, and a boss, often in the same night.

As exhausting and exhilarating as it can be, youth work is also a sacred calling. You get to walk alongside people at one of the most important stages of life. In other words, we see you. We *are* you.

Even though the high-profile moments are what generate the most enthusiasm, some of the most important work you do happens in those one-on-one conversations. So much of what you do is about establishing trust, creating a culture of welcome, and demonstrating integrity in relationships in the name of showing God's unending love to your students.

This is what you're called to do, and that is why you are the perfect person to walk alongside LGBTQ+ students during these beautiful, complicated, and overwhelming teen years. You'll make mistakes, but you'll also make a real difference. Trust that you have been empowered and equipped by the Holy Spirit to be a caring, affirming presence in their life. God has given you all the tools you need to be the kind of strong and grace-filled adult they so desperately need.

> [God] has told you, O mortal, what is good;
> and what does the Lord require of you
> but to do justice, and to love kindness,
> and to walk humbly with your God?
>
> —Micah 6:8

GLOSSARY

advocate: 1 *noun* : A person who actively works to end intolerance, educate others, and support social equity for a marginalized group. **2** *verb* : to actively support or plea in favor of a particular cause; the action of working to end intolerance or educate others.

agender: Having no (or very little) connection to the traditional system of gender, no personal alignment with the concepts of either man or woman, and/or seeing oneself as existing without gender. Sometimes called "gender neutrois," "gender neutral," or "genderless."

ally: A person who is not LGBTQ+ but shows support for LGBTQ+ people and promotes equality in a variety of ways.

androgynous: Identifying and/or presenting as neither distinguishably masculine nor distinguishably feminine.

aromantic: Experiencing little or no romantic attraction to others and/or having a lack of interest in romantic relationships/behavior. Aromanticism exists on a continuum from people who experience no romantic attraction or have no desire for romantic activities, to those who experience low levels, or romantic attraction only under specific conditions. Many of these different places on the continuum have their own identity labels (see *demiromantic*). Sometimes abbreviated to "aro" (pronounced like "arrow").

asexual: The lack of a sexual attraction or desire for other people.

binder: An undergarment used to alter or reduce the appearance of one's breasts (worn similarly to how one wears a sports bra).

biphobia: Prejudice, fear, or hatred directed toward bisexual people.

bisexual: Emotionally, romantically, or sexually attracted to more than one sex, gender, or gender identity, though not necessarily simultaneously, in the same way, or to the same degree.

cisgender: Sometimes shortened to "cis." A term used to describe a person whose gender identity aligns with that typically associated with the sex assigned to them at birth.

closeted: Describes an LGBTQ+ person who has not disclosed their sexual orientation or gender identity.

coming out: The process by which a person first acknowledges, accepts, and appreciates their sexual orientation or gender identity and begins to share that with others.

conversion therapy: Attempting to change a person's sexual orientation or gender identity through religious or psychological intervention.

cross-dresser: Someone who wears clothes of another gender/sex.

drag king: Someone who performs (hyper-) masculinity theatrically.

drag queen: Someone who performs (hyper-) femininity theatrically.

feminine-of-center; masculine-of-center: A phrase that indicates a range in terms of gender identity and expression for people who present, understand themselves, and/or relate to others in a generally more feminine/masculine way but don't necessarily identify as women or men. Feminine-of-center individuals may also identify as "femme," "submissive," "transfeminine," etc.; masculine-of-center individuals may also often identify as "butch," "stud," "aggressive," "boi," "transmasculine," etc.

femme: Someone who identifies themselves as feminine, whether it be physically, mentally, or emotionally. Often used to refer to a feminine-presenting queer person.

FtM / F2M: Female-to-male transgender or transsexual person.

gay: Emotionally, romantically, or sexually attracted to members of the same gender.

gender binary: The idea that there are only two genders and that every person is one of those two.

gender dysphoria: Clinically significant distress caused when a person's assigned birth gender is not the same as the one with which they identify. According to the American Psychiatric Association's *Diagnostic and Statistical Manual of Mental Disorders, 5th Ed.* (DSM-5), the term—which replaces "Gender Identity Disorder"—"is intended to better characterize the experiences of affected children, adolescents, and adults."

gender-expansive: Conveys a wider, more flexible range of gender identity and/or expression than typically associated with the binary gender system.

gender expression: External appearance of one's gender identity, usually expressed through behavior, clothing, haircut, or voice, and which may or may not conform to socially defined behaviors and characteristics typically associated with being either masculine or feminine.

gender-fluid: Describes a person who does not identify with a single fixed gender, or expresses a fluid or unfixed gender identity.

gender identity: One's innermost concept of self as male, female, a blend of both, or neither; how individuals perceive themselves and what they call themselves. One's gender identity can be the same as or different from their sex assigned at birth.

gender nonconforming: A broad term referring to people who do not behave in a way that conforms to the traditional expectations of their gender, or whose gender expression does not fit neatly into a category.

genderqueer: Genderqueer people typically reject notions of static categories of gender and embrace a fluidity of gender identity and often, though not always, sexual orientation. People who identify as "genderqueer" may see themselves as both male and female, neither male nor female, or falling completely outside these categories.

gender transition: The process by which some people strive to more closely align their internal knowledge of gender with its outward appearance. Some people socially transition, whereby they might begin dressing, using names and pronouns, and/or being socially recognized as another gender. Others undergo physical transitions in which they modify their bodies through medical interventions.

heteronormativity: The assumption, in individuals and/or in institutions, that everyone is heterosexual and that heterosexuality is superior to all other sexualities. Leads to invisibility and stigmatizing of other sexualities. Example: when learning a woman is married, asking her what her husband's name is. Heteronormativity also leads us to assume that only masculine men and feminine women are straight.

homophobia: The fear and hatred of or discomfort with people who are attracted to members of the same sex.

homosexual: Primarily emotionally, physically, and/or sexually attracted to members of the same sex/gender. This medical term is considered stigmatizing (particularly as a noun) due to its historical use as a category of mental illness, and is discouraged for common use (use "gay" or "lesbian" instead).

intersex: An umbrella term used to describe a wide range of natural bodily variations. In some cases, these traits are visible at birth; in others, they are not apparent until puberty. Some chromosomal variations of this type may not be physically apparent at all.

lesbian: A woman who is emotionally, romantically, or sexually attracted to other women.

LGBTQ+: An inititialism for "lesbian, gay, bisexual, transgender, and queer." Sometimes denoted with different or additional letters.

living openly: A state in which LGBTQ+ people are comfortably out about their sexual orientation or gender identity, where and when it feels appropriate to them.

MtF / M2F: male-to-female transgender or transsexual person.

nonbinary: An adjective describing a person who does not identify exclusively as a man or a woman. Nonbinary people may identify as being both a man and a woman, somewhere in between, or falling completely outside these categories. While many also identify as transgender, not all nonbinary people do.

outing: Exposing someone's lesbian, gay, bisexual, or transgender identity to others without their permission. Outing someone can have serious repercussions on employment, economic stability, personal safety, and/or religious and family situations.

pansexual: Describes someone who has the potential for emotional, romantic, or sexual attraction to people of any gender, though not necessarily simultaneously, in the same way, or to the same degree.

passing: Trans people being accepted as, or able to "pass for," a member of their self-identified gender identity (regardless of sex assigned at birth) without being identified as trans.

QPOC / QTPOC: Initialisms that stand for "queer people of color" and "queer and/or trans people of color."

queer: A term people often use to express fluid identities and orientations. Often used interchangeably with "LGBTQ+."

questioning: A term used to describe people who are in the process of exploring their sexual orientation or gender identity.

sex assigned at birth: The sex (male or female) given to a child at birth, most often based on the child's external anatomy. This is also referred to as "assigned sex at birth."

sexual orientation: An inherent or immutable enduring emotional, romantic, or sexual attraction to other people.

trans: An umbrella term covering a range of identities that transgress socially defined gender norms. Trans with an asterisk is often used in written forms (not spoken) to indicate that you are referring to the larger group nature of the term, and specifically including nonbinary identities as well as transgender men (transmen) and transgender women (transwomen).

transgender: An umbrella term for people whose gender identity and/or expression is different from cultural expectations based on the sex they were assigned at birth. Being transgender does not imply any specific sexual orientation. Therefore, transgender people may identify as straight, gay, lesbian, bisexual, etc.

transman: An identity label sometimes adopted by female-to-male transgender people or transsexuals to signify that they are men while still acknowledging their female sex at birth (sometimes referred to as "transguy").

transphobia: The fear and hatred of, or discomfort with, transgender people.

transwoman: An identity label sometimes adopted by male-to-female transgender people or transsexuals to signify that they are women while still acknowledging their male sex at birth.

two-spirit: An umbrella term traditionally within Native American communities to recognize individuals who possess qualities or fulfill roles of both genders.

ADDITIONAL RESOURCES

GENERAL LGBTQ+ ORGANIZATIONS AND RESOURCES

* GLAAD: glaad.org/resourcelist
* The Trevor Project: thetrevorproject.org
* Gay, Lesbian & Straight Education Network (GLSEN): glsen.org
* PFLAG: pflag.org For parents, family, and friends of LGBTQ+
* COLAGE: colage.org For families with one or more LGBTQ+ caregivers or parent
* It Gets Better Project: itgetsbetter.org
* StopBullying.gov: Information for LGBTQ+ youth
* Advocates for Youth (AFY): advocatesforyouth.org LGBTQ+ resources for professionals
* Gender and Sexualities Alliance (GSA) Network: gsanetwork.org
* UCLA LGBT Transgender Campus Resource Center: gbt.ucla.edu
* *Queerfully and Wonderfully Made: A Guide for LGBTQ+ Christian Teenagers*, Leigh Finke
* *This Is a Book for Parents of Gay Kids: A Question & Answer Guide to Everyday Life.* D. Owens-Reid, K. Russo, L. Stone Fish
* *Coming Out, Coming Home: Helping Families Adjust to a Gay or Lesbian Child.* Michael LaSala

BIAS

* Harvard Implicit Association Test: implicit.harvard.edu
* *The Church of Us vs. Them: Freedom from a Faith That Feeds on Making Enemies* by David E. Fitch
* *Blindspot: Hidden Biases of Good People* by Mahzarin R. Banaji
* *Thinking, Fast and Slow* by Daniel Kahnemann

- *The Person You Mean to Be: How Good People Fight Bias* by Dolly Chugh
- *Everyday Bias: Identifying and Navigating Unconscious Judgments in Our Daily Lives* by Howard J. Ross
- *The Righteous Mind: Why Good People Are Divided by Politics and Religion* by Jonathan Haidt

CHANGE/CONVERSION THERAPY

- Conversion Therapy Research: The Trevor Project: trevorproject.org
- "The Lies and Dangers of Efforts to Change Sexual Orientation or Gender Identity" hrc.org
- "Born Perfect: The Facts about Conversion Therapy," National Center for Lesbian Rights
- "Conversion Therapy and LGBT Youth: Update" by Williams Institute williamsinstitute.law.ucla.edu
- *Boy Erased: A Memoir.* Garrard Conley
- *Space at the Table: Conversations between an Evangelical Theologian and His Gay Son.* Brad and Drew Harper
- *Anything but Straight: Unmasking the Scandals and Lies behind the Ex-Gay Myth.* Wayne Besen
- *How to Survive a Summer.* Nick White
- *The Inheritance of Shame.* Peter Gajdics
- *The Straight Line: How the Fringe Science of Ex-Gay Therapy Reoriented Sexuality.* Tom Waidzunas

CHURCH LIFE AND CLERGY LIFE

- *Our Strangely Warmed Hearts: Coming Out into God's Call* Karen Oliveto (2018)
- *A Gracious Heresy: The Queer Calling of an Unlikely Prophet* Connie Tuttle (2018)
- *Being Called, Being Gay: Discernment for Ministry in the Episcopal Church* Gregory Millikin (2018)

- *Solus Jesus: A Theology of Resistance* Emily Swan and Ken Wilson (2018)
- *queering lent* slats (2017)
- *Struggling in Good Faith: LGBTQI Inclusion from 13 American Religious Perspectives* Mychal Copeland, D'vorah Rose, Ani Zonneveld (2016)
- *Reforming Sodom: Protestants and the Rise of Gay Rights* Heather Rachelle White (2015)
- *A Disreputable Priest: Being Gay in Anti-Gay Cultures* Ian Corbett (2015)
- *Does Jesus Really Love Me? A Gay Christian's Pilgrimage in Search of God in America* Jeff Chu (2014)
- *Peculiar Faith: Queer Theology for Christian Witness* Jay Emerson Johnson (2014)
- *Queer Clergy: A History of Gay and Lesbian Ministry in American Protestantism* R. W. Holmen (2014)
- *Queering Christianity: Finding a Place at the Table for LGBTQI Christians* Robert Everett Shore-Goss, Thomas Bohache, Patrick S. Cheng, Ramona Faye West (2013)

HOMELESSNESS

For immediate help:

- The National Runaway Safeline: 1-800-RUNAWAY (800-786-2929). Provides advice and resources, like shelter, transportation, assistance in finding counseling, and transitioning back to home life. Frontline staff will also act as advocates and mediators if/as needed.
- True Colors United: truecolorsunited.org (212)-461-4401 Working to end homelessness specifically among LGBTQ teens.
- National Safe Place: www.nationalsafeplace.org. Click on their "Find a Safe Place" tab to enter your zip code and

find local help. To use TXT 4 HELP, text the word "safe" and your current location (city/state/zip) to 4HELP (44357). You will receive a message with the closest Safe Place site and phone number for the local youth agency. You will also have the option to text interactively with a professional for more help. It's quick, easy, safe, and confidential.

★ National Clearinghouse on Homeless Youth & Families: 833-GET-RHYi (833-438-7494) or GetRHYi@NCHYF.org.

★ Basic Center Program: provides up to 21 days of shelter, food, clothing, and medical care; individual, group, and family counseling; crisis intervention, recreation programs, and aftercare services for teens under 18.

RESOURCES FOR YOUTH HOMELESSNESS

★ Transitional Living Program (TLP): https://www.acf.hhs.gov/fysb/programs/runaway-homeless-youth/programs/transitional-living Provides long-term residential services to homeless youth between the ages of 16 and 22. Housing may be in host families, supervised apartments, group homes (or maternity group homes). Offers educational and life skills programs.

★ Covenant House: LGBTQ Youth and Homelessness: covenanthouse.org/homeless-issues/lgbtq-homeless-youth

★ HRC's Report on LGBTQ Youth Homelessness: www.hrc.org

★ The Trevor Project's page on Youth Homelessness: thetrevorproject.org

★ "Missed Opportunities: LGBTQ Youth Homelessness in America" on Voices of Youth Count: voicesofyouthcount.org

LOCAL LGBTQ+ COMMUNITIES

* Bisexual Resource Center's list of bi communities: biresource.org/find-a-bi-group/

* CenterLink: The Community of LGBT Centers: lgbtcenters.org Enter your address or location and find your nearest LGBT community center.

* GSA Network: Your school, or a school near you, may have a Gay-Straight Alliance. Ask a school counselor or look on gsanetwork.org to locate a registered GSA near you.

* Consortium of Higher Education: LGBT Resource Professionals. www.lgbtcampus.org Scan their map to find one of their local LGBT centers on college campuses, run by at least one professional staff or graduate assistant.

* Everyone Is Gay: everyoneisgay.com Check out their "Community and Activism" page under the Resources tab for advice on finding local communities of LGBTQ young adults.

* Social media: Facebook, Instagram, or Tumblr can be good places to meet local LGBTQ people. However, always use caution and wisdom when talking to people online. Never meet up alone with someone you "met" online.

MARRIAGE AND SEXUALITY

* *Modern Kinship: A Queer Guide to Christian Marriage* David and Constantino Khalaf (2018)

* *Good Christian Sex: Why Chastity Isn't the Only Option—And Other Things the Bible Says about Sex* Bromleigh McCleneghan (2016)

* *Damaged Goods: New Perspectives on Christian Purity* Dianna Anderson (2015)

- *Sexuality and the Sacred, Second Edition: Sources for Theological Reflection* Marvin Ellison and Kelly Brown Douglas (2010)

- *Beyond Shame: Creating a Healthy Sex Life on Your Own Terms* Matthias Roberts (2019)

- *Just Love: A Framework for Christian Sexual Ethics* Margaret Farley (2008)

- *Embodiment: An Approach to Sexuality and Christian Theology* James Nelson (1978)

MEMOIR, BIOGRAPHIES, AND COMMUNITY STORIES

- *One Coin Found: How God's Love Stretches to the Margins* Emmy Kegler (2019)

- Refocusing My Family Amber Cantorna (2019)

- *Undivided: Coming Out, Becoming Whole, and Living Free from Shame* Vicky Beeching (2018)

- *Given Up for You: A Memoir of Love, Belonging, and Belief* Erin White (2018)

- *Refocusing My Family: Coming Out, Being Cast Out, and Discovering the True Love of God* Amber Cantorna (2017)

- *Our Witness: The Unheard Stories of LGBT+ Christians* Brandon Robertson (November 2017)

- *Space at the Table: Conversations between an Evangelical Theologian and His Gay Son* Brad and Drew Harper (2016)

- *Facing the Music: My Story* Jennifer Knapp (2014)

- *Loves God Likes Girls: A Memoir* Sally Gary (2013)

- *Torn: Rescuing the Gospel from the Gays-vs.-Christians Debate* Justin Lee (2013)

MENTAL HEALTH

10 COMMON WARNING SIGNS
OF A MENTAL HEALTH CONDITION:

1. Feeling sad or lack of desire to be around others, lasting for more than two weeks

2. Seriously considering or making plans to harm or kill oneself

3. Out-of-control, risky behavior

4. Sudden, overwhelming fear for no rational reason

5. Appetite suppression, throwing up, or using laxatives to lose weight; significant weight loss or weight gain

6. Seeing, hearing, or believing things that aren't real

7. Consistently using drugs or alcohol

8. Drastic mood changes, behavioral/personality swings, or poor sleeping habits

9. Extreme difficulty concentrating or staying still

10. Intense worries or fears that inhibit daily activity

MENTAL HEALTH BOOKS FOR TEENS

★ *Feeling Better: A CBT Workbook for Teens: Essential Skills and Activities to Help You Manage Moods, Boost Self-Esteem, and Conquer Anxiety.* Rachel L. Hutt, PhD

★ *Just as You Are: A Teen's Guide to Self-Acceptance & Lasting Self-Esteem.* Michelle Skeen, PsyD, and Kelly Skeen

★ *Don't Let Your Emotions Run Your Life for Teens: Dialectical Behavior Therapy Skills for Helping You Manage Mood Swings, Control Angry Outbursts, and Get Along with Others.* Sheri Van Dijk, MSW

★ *The Anxiety and Phobia Workbook: A Guide through Understanding and Dealing with Anxiety, OCD, and PTSD.* Edward Bourne, PhD

★ *My Anxious Mind: A Teen's Guide to Managing Anxiety and Panic.* Michael A. Tompkins, PhD, and Katherine A. Martinez, PsyD, illustrated by Michael Sloan

MOVIES/DOCUMENTARIES

★ *Out of Order* (2018) A documentary revealing struggles faced by LGBTQ faith.

★ *Ending the Silence* (2018). One hour documentary about sexual shame, patriarcy, and anti-LGBTQ+ teachings of the church.

★ *Love the Sinner* (2017) 15-minute documentary exploring the connection between Christianity and homophobia in the wake of the shooting at Pulse Nightclub in Orlando.

★ *Transfigurations: Transgressing Gender in the Bible* (2017). Preview available on Vimeo.

★ *Here I Am* (2016) A 30-minute series of stories of coming out and being a Christian. Available on Vimeo.

★ *Holler If You Hear Me: Black & Gay in the Church* A 2015 documentary providing an inside look at the LGBT community in the Black church. Available on BET.com.

★ *Blackbird* (2014) Tells the fictional story of a black Christian teenage boy. Available on Netflix.
The New Black (2013) A documentary that examines how African-American voters have become bitterly divided on the issue of gay marriage because of homophobia rampant in the Black church. Available for streaming on Netflix.

★ *Voices of Witness: Out of the Box* (2012) A 30-minute documentary giving voice to transgender people of faith. Available on YouTube.

★ *The Wise Kids* (2011) A film exploring the lives and faith of three youth group kids suddenly faced with their understandings and beliefs about sexuality. Available for streaming on Netflix.

- *Pariah* (2011) A young Black lesbian tries to balance her personal acceptance of her sexuality with the closeted life she lives with her Christian family. Available for streaming on Netflix.

- *Through My Eyes* (2010) The stories of young Christians who have been part of their churches' discussions on their sexual orientation and gender identity. Available on YouTube at the link above.

- *Fish Out of Water* (2009) A documentary discussing the seven "clobber verses" with pastors who support and pastors who oppose same-gender relationships. View the trailer online.

- *For the Bible Tells Me So* (2007) A documentary following five American families through the process of a child's coming out and coming to terms with faith. Available for streaming on Netflix.

- *Brother Outsider: The Life of Bayard Rustin* (2003) A documentary telling the story of Bayard Rustin, a gay Christian civil rights activist who was instrumental in coordinating the March on Washington in 1963 and was a close friend of Martin Luther King Jr. Available on PBS.org.

NATIONAL LGBTQ COMMUNITIES

FOR TEENS

- The Trevor Project: leading national organization in crisis intervention, suicide prevention, resources, and support systems for LGBTQ youth.

- It Gets Better Project: itgetsbetter.org. Inspiring stories from LGBTQ youth and adults.

- The Tribe Wellness Community: support.therapytribe. com/lgbt-support-group/ LGBTribe Members: peer-to-peer support group for LGBTQ individuals dealing with mental health issues.

- Gay, Lesbian & Straight Education Network (GLSEN): Find your local chapter or take a dive through their wonderful online resources.

- ★ LGBTQ Student Resources and Support: resource page on accreditedschoolsonline.org
- ★ Point Foundation: pointfoundation.org The national LGBTQ scholarship fund. Resources for rising college students.
- ★ Safe Schools Coalition: safeschoolscoalition.org A public-private partnership to support LGBTQ youth.
- ★ National Center for Transgender Equality (NCTE) transequality.org. Resources, self-help guides, info about transgender people, and more.
- ★ Sylvia Rivera Law Project: srlp.org legal organization that fights discrimination based on sexuality, gender expression, race, income, etc.
- ★ BiNet USA: binetusa.org America's oldest advocacy organization for bisexual, pansexual, fluid, queer-identified, and unlabeled people.
- ★ The Asexual Visibility & Education Network: asexuality.org an online community and archive of resources on asexuality.

FOR THE POLITICALLY PASSIONATE

- ★ Human Rights Campaign (HRC): Latest news, research, and resources on LGBTQ rights and activism.
- ★ Equality Federation: equalityfederation.org An organization that partners with state-based organizations that advocate for LGBTQ people.
- ★ National LGBTQ Task Force: thetaskforce.org. Advocacy opportunities, news, conference updates, and more on LGBTQ rights.

COMMUNITIES FOR PARENTS OF LGBTQ TEENS

- ★ PFLAG pfglag.org
- ★ The Center. Gaycenter.org.
- ★ Harbor. Online Support Program for Christian Parents of LGBTQ Kids: harborhere.com

- ★ Embracing the Journey: www.embracingthejourney.org
- ★ Freed Hearts: freedhearts.org/about
- ★ Parent Connect: Groups and Events for Parents of LGBTQ+ Children northpoint.org
- ★ Strong Family Alliance: strongfamilyalliance.org
- ★ Free Mom Hugs freemomhugs.org
- ★ Gender Odyssey: genderodyssey.org

ONLINE LGBTQ+ FAITH COMMUNITIES

- ★ Queer Theology: queertheology.com
- ★ Q Christian Fellowship: qchristian.org
- ★ Institute for Welcoming Resources: welcomingresources.org
- ★ Acting Out Loud: religiousinstitute.org/projects/acting-out-loud/
- ★ The Reformation Project: reformationproject.org
- ★ Center for LGBTQ and Gender Studies in Religion: clgs.org/
- ★ Human Rights Campaign's Religion & Faith section: hrc.org/explore/topic/religion-faith
- ★ Inclusive Orthodoxy: inclusiveorthodoxy.org/
- ★ Love Boldly: loveboldy.net
- ★ TransFaith: transfaithonline.org

PASTORAL CARE

- ★ *Beyond a Binary God: A Theology for Trans* Allies* Tara K. Soughers (2018)
- ★ *Ministry among God's Queer Folk: LGBT Pastoral Care* David Kundtz (2007)

QUEER THEOLOGY

- ★ *Queer Theology: Beyond Apologetics* Linn Marie Tonstad (2018)

* *Outside the Lines* Mihee Kim-Kort (2018)
* *Queer Virtue: What LGBTQ People Know about Life and Love and How It Can Revitalize Christianity* Liz Edman (2017)
* *The Courage to Be Queer* Jeff Hood (2015)
* *That We Might Become God: The Queerness of Creedal Christianity* Andy Buechel (2015)
* *Queer Christianities: Lived Religion in Transgressive Forms* Kathleen T. Talvacchia, Mark Larrimore, Michael F. Pettinger (2014)

SEXUAL ABUSE

HOTLINES, HELPLINES

* RAINN (Rape, Abuse & Incest National Network). The nation's largest anti-sexual violence organization. Call their free, confidential hotline 800-656-HOPE (4673).
* GLBTQ Domestic Violence Project: 800-832-1901. Website, info, and hotline for LGBTQ victims of domestic violence and their families.
* The Network/La Red: 617-742-4911: Emotional support, information, and safety planning for those being partner-abused or who have been abused in LGBTQ community, as well as SM or polyamorous communities.
* National Teen Dating Abuse Helpline: 1-866-331-9474
* National Domestic Violence Hotline: 1-800-799-7233 or 1-800-7870-3224 (TTY)
* National Coalition of Anti-Violence Programs: 1-212-714-1141. Links to National Advocacy for Local LGBT Communities.
* National AIDS Hotline: English: 1-800-342-2437. Spanish: 1-800-344-7432. TTY service for the deaf: 1-800-243-7889.
* Anti-Violence Project: 212-714-1141.
* National Child Abuse Hotline: 1-800 4-A-Child or 1-800-422-4453 childhelp.org/
* Darkness to Light: End Child Sexual Abuse d2l.org/

* DayOne: Partnering with youth to end dating abuse and domestic violence. Additional resources for LGBTQ youth struggling with partner abuse. dayoneny.org/

ONLINE RESOURCES FOR SEXUAL ABUSE

* NCTSN (The National Child Traumatic Stress Network): Find resources on sexual abuse, the effects, interventions, and help at www.nctsn.org
* National Coalition of Anti-Violence Programs: https://avp.org/
* 1in6.org: National helpline for men who were sexually abused or assaulted.
* VAW.net (Violence Against Women): A project of the National Resource Center on Domestic Violence.
* Invisible Girls Thrive: www.invisiblegirlsthrive.org. Honors teen girls and young women who have survived incest and all sexual abuse through "thriverships," opportunity, and education.
* RAINN rainn.org
* HRC.org: Sexual Assault and the LGBTQ Community
* Sisters of Color Ending Sexual Assault (SCESA) http://sisterslead.org/
* Trauma Center at Justice Resource Institute: traumacenter.org/

BOOKS ON SEXUAL ABUSE/FOR SEXUAL ABUSE VICTIMS

* *Helping Victims of Sexual Abuse* by Lynn Heitritter & Jeanette Vought
* *Healing the Ravaged Soul: Tending the Spiritual Wounds of Child Sexual Abuse* by Sue Magrath
* *The Child Safeguarding Policy Guide for Churches and Ministries* by Basyle Tchividijian & Shira Berkovitis
* *Where Was God? Spiritual Questions of Sexually Abused Children* by Barbara Hughes

- *Healing from the Trauma of Childhood Sexual Abuse: The Journey for Women.* Karen A. Duncan
- *Queering Sexual Violence: Radical Voices from within the Anti-Violence Movement.* Edited by Jennifer Patterson
- *Written on the Body: Letters from Trans and Non-Binary Survivors of Sexual Assault and Domestic Violence.* Edited by Lexi Bean

SEX EDUCATION

- American Sexual Health Association (ASHA): ashasexualhealth.org
- Our Whole Lives: Lifespan Sexuality Education (OWL)
- Scarleteen: Sex Ed for the Real World. scarleteen.com
- Planned Parenthood: plannedparenthood.org Check out their LGBTQ section under the "Teen" tab.
- Talk with Your Kids: talkwithyourkids.org/
- Sexuality Education on Religious Institute: religiousinstitute.org/issue/sexuality-education/
- Center for Young Women's Health. youngwomenshealth.org
- Young Men's Health. youngmenshealthsite.org
- "Queering Sexual Education" on teenhealthsource.com Article and video links for sex ed for queer teens.

SEXUAL ORIENTATION AND SCRIPTURE— BY LGBTQ PEOPLE

- *Gay & Christian, No Contradiction: A Brief Guide for Reconciling Christian Faith & LGBT+ Identity* Brandan Robertson (2017)
- *God and the Gay Christian: The Biblical Case in Support of Same-Sex Relationships* Matthew Vines (2015)
- *Quench! Refreshing Devotionals by Gay, Trans, and Affirming Christians* Rev. Keith J. Phillips (ed), (2009)

* *Bulletproof Faith: A Spiritual Survival Guide for Gay and Lesbian Christians* Candace Chellew-Hodge, (2008)
* *Reconciling Journey: A Devotional Workbook for Lesbian and Gay Christians* Michal Anne Pepper, (2003)
* *Blessed Bi Spirit: Bisexual People of Faith* Debra Kolodney (ed), (2000)

SEXUAL ORIENTATION AND SCRIPTURE—BY ALLIES

* *UnClobber: Rethinking Our Misuse of the Bible on Homosexuality* Colby Martin (2016)
* *The Bible's Yes to Same-Sex Marriage: An Evangelical's Change of Heart* Mark Achtemeier (2014)
* *Walking the Bridgeless Canyon: Repairing the Breach between the Church and the LGBT Community* Kathy Baldock (2014)
* *Changing Our Mind: The Landmark Call for Inclusion of LGBTQ Christians* David P. Gushee (2014)
* *The Bible Tells Me So: Why Defending Scripture Has Made Us Unable to Read It* Peter Enns (2014)
* *UNFAIR: Christians and the LGBT Question* John Shore (2013)
* *Bible, Gender, Sexuality: Reframing the Church's Debate on Same-Sex Relationships* James Brownson (2013)
* *Sexuality in the New Testament: Understanding the Key Texts* William Loader (2010)
* *Jesus, the Bible, and Homosexuality, Revised and Expanded Edition: Explode the Myths, Heal the Church* Jack Rogers (2009)
* *Sex and the Single Savior: Gender and Sexuality in Biblical Interpretation* Dale Martin (2006)

SUBSTANCE ABUSE

Signs of substance abuse in teens:
* hanging out with different friends
* not caring about your appearance

* getting worse grades in school
* missing classes or skipping school
* losing interest in your favorite activities
* getting in trouble in school or with the law
* having different eating or sleeping habits
* having more problems with family members and friends

When considering the best treatment for someone:
* Know that treatments are all different and unique to each person.
* Know that quitting substance abuse is extremely difficult, even if they want to.
* Symptoms of detox may include depression, anxiety, and other mood disorders, as well as restlessness and sleeplessness. Treatment centers will keep the youth safe and comfortable through this process.
* Relapsing doesn't mean that treatment failed.
* Treatment requires major, often difficult lifestyle changes. Setbacks are to be expected. Keep persevering through them and consider a different treatment method to replace unsuccessful methods.
* Know that your treatment providers will keep your information confidential. They are not under obligation to tell your parents or law enforcement about your drug use unless you are in danger of harming yourself or someone else.

To find immediate help:
* PRIDE Institute: 888-616-5031. pride-institute.com Recovery programs provide solutions for all types of substance abuse, trauma, sexual and behavioral issues.
* SAMHSA (Substance Abuse and Mental Health Services Administration): 1-800-662-HELP (4357). Free, confidential, 24/7, 365-day-a-year treatment referral and

information service for individuals and families facing mental and/or substance use disorders.

RESOURCES

- ✦ Recovery Is Possible: therecoveryvillage.com
- ✦ Addiction Center addictioncenter.com
- ✦ "Drug Rehab Programs for Teens and Young Adults" on American Addiction Centers https://americanaddictioncenters.org/rehab-guide/teens
- ✦ "Substance Use Resources for Adolescents and Young Adults" adolescenthealth.org
- ✦ National Institute on Drug Abuse for Teens teens.drugabuse.gov

SUICIDE

Please make sure that all your youth have access to these resources:

- ✦ Crisis Text Line: Text START to 741-741 to message 24/7 with a trained Crisis Counselor.
- ✦ National Suicide Hotline: 1-800-273-8255. Free, confidential support for any age at any time, 24/7.
- ✦ Trevor Project: 1-866-488-7386. The nation's leading organization for crisis intervention and suicide prevention specifically for LGBTQ young people under 25. 24/7 support line.
- ✦ Trans Lifeline: translifeline.org or call 877-565-8860. A national trans-led organization dedicated to improving the quality of trans lives.
- ✦ LGBTQ National Youth Talkline. email: help@LGBThotline.org

For someone considering non-suicidal self-harm:

- ✦ Self-Abuse Finally Ends (S.A.F.E.): 800-DONTCUT (800-366-8288) offers local support and therapy referrals as well as immediate support.

RECOGNIZING WHEN A TEEN IS SUICIDAL

Contributing causes:

* History of problems at home or school
* Low self-esteem
* Believes no one cares
* Is depressed/suffering from other mental health conditions
* Abusing alcohol or drugs
* Experienced acutely stressful life events, such as unwanted pregnancy, law trouble, not meeting high parental expectations

Warning Signs:

* Noticeable changes in eating or sleeping habits
* Irrationally severe, violent, or rebellious behavior
* Withdrawing from family or friends
* Sexual promiscuity, truancy, and vandalism
* Drastic personality changes
* Agitation, restlessness, distress, or panicky behavior
* Talking or writing about committing suicide, even jokingly
* Giving away prized possessions
* Sudden drop in school performance

TEEN SUICIDE PREVENTION RESOURCES:

* Suicide Prevention Resource Center (SPRC) www.sprc.org Crisis Line: 1-800-273-TALK (8255)
* National Institute of Mental Health (NIMH) https://www.nimh.nih.gov/health/topics/ suicide-prevention/index.shtml
* The Society for the Prevention of Teen Suicide (SPTS) www.sptsusa.org
* Centers for Disease Control and Prevention (CDC) https://www.cdc.gov/violenceprevention/suicide/ resources.html

* Action Alliance for Suicide Prevention:
  http://actionallianceforsuicideprevention.org/resources
* American Foundation for Suicide Prevention (AFSP)
  https://afsp.org/find-support/resources/
* Crisis Text Line: www.crisistextline.org
  Crisis Text Line: 741-741
* The Trevor Project: http://www.thetrevorproject.org/
  specifically for LGBTQ teens
* Society for the Prevention of Teen Suicide:
  www.sptsuse.org/teens/

Resources for Parents and Caregivers of Suicidal Teens:

* National Alliance on Mental Illness (NAMI): Can
  connect parents with support groups in their area
* Local YMCA chapters: Often have support groups for
  parents and teens
* DBSA's Balanced Mind Parents Network (Depression
  and Bipolar Support Alliance): Highly recommended
  online community for parents of suicidal teens
  https://www.dbsalliance.org/support/
* *A Parent's Guide for Suicidal and Depressed Teens: Help
  Recognizing If a Child Is in Crisis and What to Do about It:*
  Kate Williams
* *Depression and Your Child: A Guide for Parents and
  Caregivers* by Deborah Serani
* *Night Falls Fast: Understanding Suicide* by Kay Redfield
* *Grieving a Suicide: A Loved One's Search for Comfort,
  Answers, and Hope.* Albert Y. Hsu

Therapy
Brief Guide to finding the right counselor:

1. Ask friends, church staff, local LGBTQ+ communities, school
   counselors, etc. for referrals, or search online.

2. Read online profiles well; look for therapists who are LGBTQ+ or specialize in that field, and who have experience dealing with teenagers. Think about what qualities the specific teen might need.

3. Make sure that a counselor or therapist is certified. Look for "LPC" (licensed professional counselor), "LCSW" or "LSW" (licensed clinical social worker or licensed social worker). Other acronyms indicating certification in specific fields include LEP, LPCC, LMFT, LCP. Verify credentials on the Department of Consumer Affairs website for your state.

4. Remind the youth that some therapy is covered by health insurance and to check their parent's plan.

5. Remind the youth that there are many types of and approaches to therapy. If they don't like the first one they go to, encourage them to find a therapist with a different approach.

6. Encourage the youth to set up a consultation or screening call before setting up an appointment. Help them formulate questions that are important for them to find the right therapist.

7. After a few weeks, check up with the youth and see how they're feeling about therapy/counseling. If the therapist/counselor just doesn't feel like a good fit, suggest they leave and try a different one.

8. Make sure they know the warning signs of a bad therapist: therapist constantly checking watch, guilting you for quitting, threatening a spiral of depression if you stop therapy, therapist talking more than you, interrupting you often, sexually or emotionally inappropriate behavior, violation of confidentiality (the last two are reportable offenses).

Online Counseling Resources:

★ The Christian Closet: thechristiancloset.com The first fully LGBTQ team of counselors, coaches, and spiritual directors, providing 100% online mental and spiritual health services.

- pridecounseling.com. Fill out info about your orientation/identity and get matched with a licensed therapist. Messaging with your therapist is according to your schedule.
- goodtherapy.com. Check here for licensed counselors with LGBTQ experience or education.
- Psychology Today. psychologytoday.com Check out their "Finding a Gay Therapist" section and enter your city or zip code.
- The Tribe Wellness Community: support.therapytribe. com/lgbt-support-group/ LGBTribe Members: Peer-to-peer support group for LGBTQ individuals dealing with mental health issues.

FOR PARENTS

Questions to ask potential counselors

- What experience do you have with the particular problem my teen is struggling with?
- How long have you been in practice?
- Describe how you will work with my teen.
- Will other family members be involved in the therapy process?
- What license do you have, and is it current?
- How do you establish goals for therapy and measure progress?
- Are you a member of a professional organization?
- Can you explain the therapy approach you use?

TRANSGENDER AND GENDER NONCONFORMING RESOURCES

ONLINE RESOURCES:

- The National Center for Transgender Equality: transequality.org/
- Trans Lifeline: www.translifeline.org/ Hotline: 877-565-8860

- ✦ The Jim Collins Foundation: to fund gender-conforming surgeries for those who need it. jimcollinsfoundation.org/
- ✦ Trans Women of Color Collective: twocc.us/
- ✦ Transgender Law Center: transgenderlawcenter.org/
- ✦ Trans Justice Funding Project: transjusticefundingproject.org/
- ✦ Human Rights Campaign: "Explore: Transgender" hrc.org/explore/topic/transgender

BOOKS:

- ✦ *The Social Justice Advocate's Handbook: A Guide to Gender* by Sam Killerman (2013)
- ✦ *Stone Butch Blues* by Leslie Feinberg (1993, 2012)
- ✦ *Trans Bodies, Trans Selves: A Resource for the Transgender Community.* Laura Erickson-Schroth (2014)
- ✦ *The Transgender Child: A Handbook for Families and Professionals.* Stephanie A. Brill (2008)
- ✦ *Transgender History.* Susan Stryker (2017)

YOUTH SPECIFIC:

- ✦ *Where's MY Book? A Guide for Transgender and Gender Non-Conforming Youth, Their Parents, & Everyone Else.* Linda Gromko (2015)
- ✦ *Being Jazz: My Life as a (Transgender) Teen.* Jazz Jennings (2017)
- ✦ *Rethinking Normal: A Memoir in Transition.* Katie Rain Hill (2015)
- ✦ *Some Assembly Required: The Not-So-Secret Life of a Transgender Teen.* Arin Andrews (2015)
- ✦ *Tomboy: A Graphic Novel Memoir.* Liz Prince (2014)
- ✦ *Beyond Magenta: Transgender Teens Speak Out.* Susan Kuklin (2015)
- ✦ *Gender Identity: The Ultimate Teen Guide (It Happened to Me); 2nd Edition.* Cynthia L. Winfield (2019)

- *The Gender Quest Workbook: A Guide for Teens and Young Adults Exploring Gender Identity.* Testa, PhD; Coolhart PhD; Peta MA MS; Lev LCSW-R CASAC (2015)
- Trans Love edited by Freiya Benson. (2019)
- Family Specific:
- *Gender Born, Gender Made: Raising Healthy Gender-Nonconforming Children.* Diane Ehrensaft, PhD (2011)
- *Gender Outlaw: On Men, Women and the Rest of Us.* Kate Bornstein (2016)
- *Raising My Rainbow: Adventures in Raising a Fabulous, Gender Creative Son.* Lori Duron. (2013)
- *The Right to Be Out: Sexual Orientation and Gender Identity in America's Public Schools.* Stuart Biegel (2018)
- *Stuck in the Middle with You: A Memoir of Parenting in Three Genders* by Jennifer Finney (2014)
- *On the Couch with Dr. Angello: Raising & Supporting Transgender Youth* by Dr. Michele Angello (2013)
- *Transgender Family Law: A Guide to Effective Advocacy.* Jennifer Levi & Elizabeth E. Monnin-Browder (2012)
- *Transitions of the Heart.* Rachel Pepper. Written by and for mothers of trans/GNC children. (2012)
- *Two Spirits, One Heart: A Mother, Her Transgender Son, and Their Journey to Love and Acceptance.* Marsha Aizumi (2013)
- *The Gender Creative Child: Pathways for Nurturing and Supporting Children Who Live Outside Gender Boxes.* Diane Ehrensaft (2016)

TRANS/GNC IDENTITY AND FAITH

- *Transfigured: A 40-Day Journey through Scripture for Gender-Queer and Transgender People* Suzanne DeWitt Hall (2018)
- *Transforming: The Bible and the Lives of Transgender Christians* Austen Hartke (2017)

* *This Is My Body: Hearing the Theology of Transgender Christians* Christina Beardsley (2017)
* *Shattering Masks: Affirming Identity. Transitioning Faith* Laura Beth Taylor (2016)
* *Transgender, Intersex, and Biblical Interpretation* Teresa J. Hornsby and Deryn Guest (2016)
* *Sex Difference in Christian Theology: Male, Female, and Intersex in the Image of God* Megan Defranza (2015)

ENDNOTES

1   Accelerating Acceptance 2017. GLAAD

2   Lytle and Blosnich. "Association of Religiosity with Sexual Minority Suicide Ideation and Attempt," 2018.

3   The Trevor Project.

4   "The origin of the term 'intersectionality,'" *Columbia Journalism Review*.

5   Lorde, Audre, "There Is No Hierarchy of Oppression," *Bulletin: Homophobia and Education*, Council on Interracial Books for Children, 1983.

6   Intersex Society of North America

7   Yale Scientific.

8   *American Anthropology*, Margaret Mead.

9   Williams Institute

10 Human Rights Campaign

11 Tess DeCarlo. *Trans History*

12 Queer Magic, Tomas Prower

13 Human Rights Campaign

14 Human Rights Campaign

15 American Journal of Preventive Medicine

16 Centers for Disease Control and Prevention: Youth Risk Behavior Surveillance 2017

17 Trevor Project; Centers for Disease Control and Prevention

18 National Mentoring Resource Center

19 Williams Institute

20 American Psychological Association

21 American Foundation for Suicide Prevention. "Risk Factors and Warning Signs"

22 Mayo Clinic. "Suicide: What to do when someone is suicidal"

23 The Trevor Project. "Research Brief: Accepting Adults Reduce Suicide Attempts among LGBTQ Youth"

24 Covenant Eyes. Pornography Statistics

25 Williams Institute. "Gender expression, violence, and bullying victimization."

26 GLSEN. Policy Maps

27 stopbullying.gov. "What Is Cyberbullying?"

28 Human Rights Campaign. LGBTQ Youth Report

29 Except for the first statistic in the list, all data is from the Centers for Disease Control and Prevention, Youth Risk Behavior Surveillance 2017

30 Centers for Disease Control and Prevention, Youth Risk Behavior Surveillance 2017

31 National Center for Transgender Equality

32 Gender Spectrum. Transgender Students and School Bathrooms: FAQ

33 National Coalition for the Homeless. Youth Homelessness